THE GENERAL SPEAKS:
INTIMATE CONVERSATIONS WITH THE DEAD
Major General Albert N. Stubblebine III
(US Army, Deceased)
February 6, 1930 - February 6, 2017
www.GeneralBertSpeaks.com

In Collaboration With
Rima E. Laibow, MD
Ralph Fucetola, JD, Editor

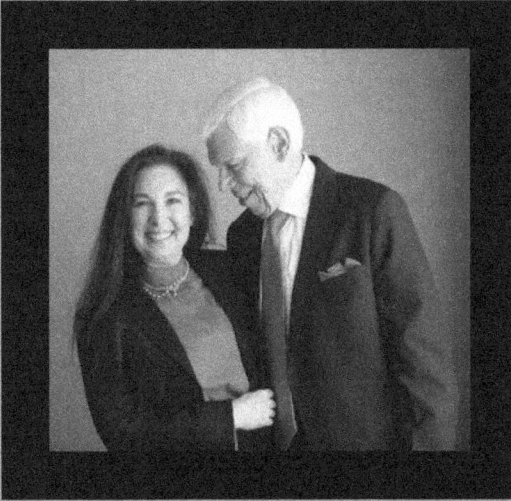

Dr. Rima and General Bert
© 2017 – 2020

First Printing: 01 January 2020
Through www.LuLu.com

ISBN: 978-1-79484-335-6

THE GENERAL SPEAKS

INDEX

INTRODUCTION

To all appearances, Major General Albert N. Stubblebine III died in the Intensive Care Unit of Robert Wood Johnson University Hospital on his 87th birthday. Causes of death are listed as "Acute Myocardial Infarction", "Pleural Effusion", "Respiratory Failure" and "Sepsis".

My name is Rima E. Laibow, MD. General Bert and I were together for nearly 26 years and married for 23 of them. I was with him as he struggled – hard - not to die but finally did succumb following two Code Blue events (cardiac arrests) the evening prior and several more on that day – his 87th birthday.

There is no doubt about it: General Bert's body irrefutably died and was subsequently irrefutably destroyed through cremation.

General Bert's consciousness and energy, however, did not die. He began making his clear and conscious presence known starting two days after his physical death when he arranged for a psychic intermediary (of whom I had never heard) to call me on a phone not listed anywhere in my name, in my fresh grief and give me very specific and particular information to assure me that he was, if not alive and well, still very well, indeed.

Seven days after that, on February 15, 2017, General Bert produced his first medically verified "miracle" cure leaving a senior Columbia University retinal surgeon confirming the events without any explanation for the complete and inexplicable cure of the well-documented progressive, irreversible condition which had been leading toward my total blindness for the past 5 years.

Despite my deep skepticism, I knew that the information from the first intermediary was specific to General Bert and was strikingly authentic. The psychic intermediary asked for, and received absolutely nothing for her generous sharing of General Bert's information so there was neither gain nor glory in it for her. But, with time, her ability to move her own mind "out of the way" overtook the "transmissions" from General Bert; they were clearly less and less his awareness and, correspondingly, more and more hers.

Deeply frustrated by this deterioration, I went on a search for a better intermediary, a clearer conduit. It was a maddeningly frustrating search. Not finding anyone to serve as a better intermediary, in a frustrated rage, I took on that role and began opening myself up to "hear" what

General Bert had to "say" on a daily basis sitting at the computer keyboard.

Ralph Fucetola, JD, our dear friend and Co-Trustee of the Natural Solutions Foundation, has been an open minded and open-hearted student of such possibilities for decades making him a perfect companion in this exploration. Ralph has joined me less frequently but with similar results in connecting directly with Bert and we often "triangulate" information by asking the same question without sharing the results until we both had completed the assignment. Occasionally a very few others participate in this small experimental group.

The alignments in the material we receive are striking and startling. The questions we put to General Bert often have no meaning or context to any but the person posing the question, yet the answers align astonishingly well, consistently. The differences are in the vocabulary which is more personal when the conversation is with me and more formal with other people.

Much to my astonishment, I realized that I was receiving information, some of which could be my production, but much of which could not. In addition, General Bert has generously made physical, observable and measurable changes visible to me and others including, for example, an otherwise medically impossible shift of my eye color from solid brown to light hazel with gold rays emanating from the pupil. General Bert, as you might guess, had light hazel eyes with gold rays emanating from the pupil.

General Bert's Light Hazel Eyes, 2014, Santiago, Chile

That was to illustrate the meaning of his repeated assertion to me that "We are one". When I told him that was delightfully poetic but I did not know what it actually meant, I awoke the next morning to find that my eyes were now *his* eyes, at least aesthetically.

I took the trouble of confirming with an ophthalmologist what I already knew as a physician: no cause of bilateral, overnight and dramatic change of eye color is known which is not associated with immediate blindness. I did not go blind.

My 2008 Passport picture with brown eyes

My 2019 Passport photo with hazel eyes

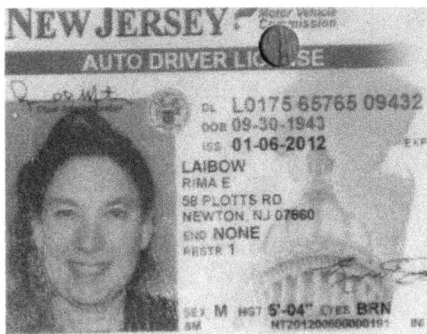

New Jersey License issued 2012 indicates brown eyes

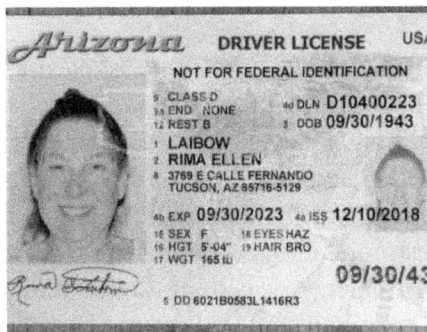

Arizona License issued 2018 indicates hazel eyes

This has helped me greatly and apparently helped others, too, in coming to grips with the actual nature of this remarkable series of transmissions.

Ralph and I both asked General Bert what he wanted this book called and he chose the title. The current volume represents a very small selection of the astonishing and on-going communication from General Bert.

The rest of the transmissions are available electronically and cover love, death, cosmology, time/space, quantum physics, genetic, energetics, and much, much more. We are making access to that ongoing experience to those who receive this book. Details ahead...

When I transcribe these transmissions, sometimes I understand them and sometimes I do not. Experts in the related areas (quantum physics, for example) find those that pertain to their specialty highly enlightening and usually groundbreaking. Like the physical manifestations (including the "impossible" sudden cure of my progressive loss of vision) these confirmations of the absolute correctness of what is incomprehensible to me are highly confirmatory of the external source of these transmissions. They may be of confirmatory significance to you, the reader, or not.

In the summer of 2017 General Bert asked me to get some art supplies. I could not imagine why, since I have no graphic abilities whatsoever. He, an engineer, was graphically skilled and asked me to download a set of remarkable drawings which made no sense to me but were of great interest, including a schematic for a totally non-polluting, fuel-free energy system, to the quantum scientists and engineers who have studied them. They are contained in the blog where his complete transmissions are posted.

No religion is being built here; no version of absolute truth is being peddled. The information is presented because we believe it is of deep significance and we are persuaded of its authenticity sufficiently to bring it forward without the use of pseudonyms or the authorship of "Anonymous".

This has been a difficult road for me personally and the willingness to trust the material, and trust its validity, has been a long and continuous one requiring, and receiving, documentation of the reality of what was coming through, and its source, from documentable and very, very high strangeness events all along this amazing road – which continue. They are all fully documented in the blog.

You do not have to agree with or value the material herein. It would be nice, however, if you were kind about whatever your thoughts are. Real people with real feelings are exposing them to you in the process of sharing this, to us, deeply precious material.

It is important to note that presented to you both in this book and in digital format is precisely what Ralph and I receive with two major exceptions.

First, Ralph and I correct typos and such minor items, but leave the sense of the transmissions unchanged, whatever our feelings about the content (For example, I have been very angry with the General and taken him to task for some particular events. His responses have been rather astonishing and not at all what I wanted or expected him to say!)

Second, when there are negative personal observations or direct conflicts as in on-going legal actions such as the ones around the nature and causes of his death, or the defrauding of General Bert's Trust (which he thoughtfully established on my behalf before his death although in good health at

the time), names and identifying details have been removed to prevent further conflict and claims of slander or liable.

Before his unnecessary, *in*tentional and untimely death (there are legal cases about that issue ongoing as I write this so the details will have to wait) General Bert was a fearless explorer of possibilities and an astonishing energy healer. He continues to be all of that, and a great deal more, since the death of his physical body. That does not preclude the fact that I miss him with aching intensity minute by minute every day without exception since his death.

In fact, I make a practice of going somewhere very different and very far away each Christmas/New Year's holiday to avoid the utterly unendurable pain of his absence from what was, under his hands and heart, a time of astonishing beauty and joy, created solely for my delight by a loving and artistic man who would create a Christmas tree like the Holiday Leonardo DaVinci or wrap a package like the Benvenuto Cellini of giftwrap.

He took special delight in doing that because, being Jewish, Christmas was outside, in stores and on streets, not in my home. Discovering that deficit, he made it a special mission to light my holiday world with astonishing creativity and beauty.

You can see why I visit the Harbin Ice Festival or India's regions over this period, which I cannot imagine surviving otherwise, frankly.

Photos of the 2019 Harbin Ice Festival

You will find that these transmissions in the Blog are both abundant and very widely varied.

This book merely serves as an introduction to them. Those who are interested in the rest of these *Intimate Conversations with the Dead* are invited to secure access to the private blog where the full transcripts of these conversations are posted as they occur. Details at the end of this book

As of November, 2019, General Bert's astounding information now exceeds 1,500 searchable pages. Much of it is a deep and wide ranging conversation between two separated lovers who continue their respectful, tender, serious, but sometimes playful, sometimes not so playful, relationship across the boundaries of apparent separation and death.

Their dialogue, and the often-startling information it contains, is sampled below. Its richness is profound.

This profound, personal, and remarkable material covers ordinary and mundane matters mixed into cosmological and metaphysical ones. General Bert and I speak openly and frankly about matters very, very large including the very nature of Reality – and beyond - and intimately small, as loving couples will. And we are still, astonishingly, a deeply loving couple, bonded in time and out of it.

Not surprisingly, General Bert and Counsel Ralph tend to focus on less intimate, and more particular thoughts and questions.

As I mentioned, questions are often put to General Bert by members of a very small circle and the answers are compared as a validation technique to reduce the risk of confabulation, imagination and guesswork. This is consistent with the Remote Viewing methodology that General Bert developed for the US Army's Strategic Intelligence Services, when he was the Commanding

General of INSCOM (US Army Intelligence and Security Command) up until his retirement in 1984.

It is important to note that many of the concepts first shared with me by General Bert made absolutely no sense to me whatsoever since I have no background in physics or quantum physics, areas in which General Bert has, since his death, apparently developed a great interest.

To deal with this rather complete lack, General Bert asked me to find a quantum physicist to review this material and selected the physicist for me to contact at a meeting he asked me to attend called "The Science of Consciousness".

That scientist is Philip L'Homedieu: his validation and exploration of the quantum physics shared by the General Bert has been of great importance to everyone involved in this amazing project.

We refer to ourselves as "General Bert's Team".

The General Speaks book and Blog includes powerful new ways of looking at the nature of Reality and the realities we all experience with General Bert's characteristic wit, wisdom, foresight and passion. Because of the nature of Probability, though, the temptation to ascribe perfect foresight and infallibility to General Bert is a mistake.

He frequently reminds me, "I am not omnipotent, just (slightly) dead."

His batting average for seeing where we are going, however, is pretty remarkable.

General Bert's Team invites you to join us for a truly unique, and constantly unfolding journey starting with this book, *"The General Speaks"*.

This book is a sampler of some of the revelations received by General Bert's Team. The source material is so astonishingly rich it has been highly challenging to decide what could possibly be left out for this introduction.

General Bert's Team decided to create a living book in active collaboration with our amazing and generous "Slightly Dead Guy" (SDG as General Bert calls himself): this introductory book opens three of the many doors in our conversations with General Bert. The others are available once you have read the book and decide that this is material you would like to access. At the end of the current volume we'll tell you how to gain access to the full body of information.

If these messages resonate with you, we invite you to join us and gain access to the ongoing dialogue. Ralph and I can assure you that whatever else your response might be, you will be amazed.

December 1, 2019

Ralph Fucetola, JD – Editor
Rima E. Laibow, MD

PS: Over time, each member of General Bert's Team has formed his/her own understanding of the origin and nature of these data. No one needs to share our understanding or assessment of these near daily transmissions and the remarkable physical evidence that supports them. We do, however, request you deal with this material respectfully and with the loss and grief of those who love/loved General Bert in his physical, animated form and continue to love him in his [very] energetic form. RF

PART ONE: PROLOGUE

The following document is the result of an unexpected, but decidedly welcome, stream of communication between Maj. Gen. Albert N. Stubblebine III (US Army, Deceased), his wife, Rima E. Laibow, MD, ("Dr. Rima") their friend and colleague, Ralph Fucetola, JD, and others.

General Bert, as he was known, collapsed on September 1, 2016 during what was intended to be a brief stay in the US to receive natural treatments for some decidedly non-lethal health issues. At that time, General Bert and Dr. Rima were staying in Santiago, Chile but legally residing in New Jersey.

Taken by ambulance to the JFK Medical Center in Edison, NJ, General Bert was diagnosed with septicemia and aspiration pneumonia. He remained in coma for days. He was hospitalized for 158 days and when the Medical Director of the hospital suddenly forbade the nutrients and food that Dr. Rima was giving General Bert, forcing him back into life-threatening extremis, we went to Court to obtain a ground breaking Court Order (in Middlesex County NJ Superior Court case C-213-16) to allow Dr. Rima to continue to provide real food and high dose, effective nutrients for him. The saga of his nutrition-facilitated recovery, Dr. Rima's and General Bert's *personal* health freedom war with the pharmaceutical system, his important legal victory and his ultimate and unnecessary death on his 87th birthday, February 6, 2017, is the subject for another book.

It is also the subject of major legal action by Dr. Rima currently in progress.

He died in Dr. Rima's arms. She was absolutely distraught with grief.

Two days after his death, a total stranger called her with "a message from General Bert". The woman, a psychic, did, indeed, deliver a message which was both intimate and specific from General Bert to Dr. Rima. There was no other identifiable source for the information, which appeared to be from General Bert.

Subsequent conversations with the psychic produced less and less specificity and more and more generality along with her obvious fantasies about a General.

Dr. Rima reached out to various other psychics, who sometimes sought to connect to General Bert as an act of kindness, sometimes as an act of income generation. In every case there was a great deal of the psychic and very little of General Bert or, worse, only the psychic's information/imagination/guess-work/standard patter, or what General Bert called, while he was studying, creating and overseeing Remote Viewing for the US Army during the 1980s, "overlay."

There were two other spontaneous messages brought to Dr. Rima's attention from well-known psychics that suggested General Bert's willingness and desire to communicate. In one case the spontaneously offered message, through Ralph Fucetola, by Rhonda, a recognized and well-known Higher Self Channel, to Dr. Rima was:

"Look for me in stillness
Look for me on the horizon."

Ralph recognized this cryptic "Poemantra" as a reference to the Remote Viewing Protocol (RV) developed and taught

by General Bert, and used by the US Army for intelligence gathering.

After one particularly frustrating (and expensive) "session" with yet another alleged psychic, Dr. Rima, both disappointed and enraged, but still encouraged by the crumbs of apparently valid communication produced over the past several months, had been typing verbatim notes of what the latest unsatisfying psychic had been saying. In complete frustration and irritation, sitting at the computer after two frustrating and expensive hours, she slammed her hands down on the keyboard, yelling in exasperation, "Damn it, I'll do it myself! *TALK TO ME, BERT!*"

To her astonishment and disbelief, apparently he did -- and he continues to do so.

She reports experiencing an inner 'knowing' of conversation, much like the interior voice of a strong memory, not hearing a voice. She felt that she was now in direct conversation with General Bert, minus any intermediary.

She began recording what she 'heard" and experienced and found that although she was filled with questions and skepticism, doubt and disbelief, there was enough specific, verifiable information not previously known to her – or knowable by her - emerging through this means of communication that was incontrovertible that she determined to continue reaching out to her beloved husband.

For example, specific quantum physics terminology was used properly although she had no knowledge of that topic and had no idea what the meaning of these discussions might be.

Just 11 days after General Bert's death, Dr. Rima experienced a medically documented, inexplicable and totally unexpected resolution of a serious and irreversible retinal condition. The prognosis offered by several specialists was the same: total blindness. This serious problem had been documented and progressing since 2012.

General Bert was a powerful energy healer with a conviction that there was nothing that could not be healed with strong Intentionality. He had a remarkable track record to support that belief. He was – and is - also fiercely protective of Dr. Rima.

Here is a link to General Bert's Healing Meditation. It is taken from a presentation he made in 2010 and was used by Dr. Rima and General Bert repeatedly during his long hospitalization.

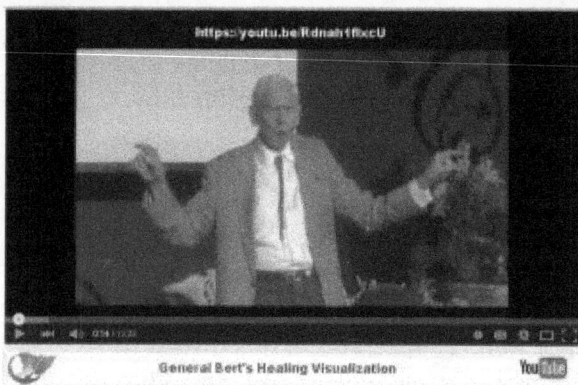

General Bert's Healing Visualization

https://yout
u.be/Rdnah1flxcU

As Dr. Rima struggled to come to grips with whether she was confabulating this material, General Bert often urged her to remember the seemingly impossible sudden resolution of the threat to her vision. "Eyes, Woman, Eyes!" he would say.

That is referenced in the material contained in this document.

Dr. Rima began setting aside time daily at the computer to reach out to General Bert. Her process was simple: using a font in one color [blue], she would type out her thoughts and questions, share daily events and other intimacies of a couple's life together by typing on the computer while meditative music played in the background.

She would then close her eyes, go into an altered state and "listen" for the inner experience and type it exactly as she heard it. Because the dominant brain wave frequency of such states is lower than that of normal waking consciousness, sometimes she would appear to fall asleep and would return to the process the next day.

These communications continue actively between General Bert and Dr. Rima.

What follows is an excerpted version of those daily communications. While absolutely true to the content presented, it has been edited for spelling, punctuation and other technical matters since Dr. Rima records her experience while typing at the computer in an altered state with her eyes closed.

They have also been edited to remove what would be, to the casual reader, highly repetitious discussions of Dr. Rima's profound grief, longing, loneliness and the deep love that she and General Bert had, and have, for one another. Identifying references to specific people have been removed as well, but intimate references that would be appropriately shared by a couple, as General Bert and Dr. Rima were for nearly 26 years (and still are), as you will see, remain.

Their friend, companion and Natural Solutions Foundation Co-Trustee, Ralph Fucetola, JD, has a long and widely ranging history of exploration of these areas between the obvious 'known' and the subtle 'unknown' so when General Bert invited him to reach out to him as well, quite separate from the communication that he and Dr. Rima were sharing, Ralph took that opportunity. His contributions to the dialogue are included as well. One important aspect of General Bert's Remote Viewing Protocol is the use of multiple viewers to cross check the validity of the information received.

Both Ralph and Rima sometimes bring the same question or topic to General Bert's attention and then compare the information received only after both of them have had a chance to "speak" with General Bert. Ralph's process for reaching out to Bert is slightly different, but similar in many central aspects. He includes the use of the Signature Frequency set associated with General Bert.

It should be clearly noted that neither Ralph nor Dr. Rima can fully explain the events and strange realities presented in this chronical. But external corroboration (including, in some instances, photographic and laboratory evidence) is available for many of them and an internal sense of rightness, or lack of it, directs their efforts.

General Bert specifically indicated that both Ralph and Dr. Rima would experience "high strangeness" and as you will see, he has certainly more than kept his promise!

This information is not presented as science, religion, revealed truth or transcendent fact. It is shared as the experience of General Bert as he presents it and of Dr. Rima and Ralph as they receive it.

To all of us who say that any or all of this is impossible, we recall one of General Bert's favorite questions:

"Who made that rule?"

Transcending the rigid definitions of life and death, General Bert (who had an astonishing sense of humor) refers to himself, in the course of the cosmology that he presents, as an 'SDG', a 'Slightly Dead Guy' and refers to Dr. Rima as "My Undead Woman" and the rest of us here as "the Undead", giving, as he always has done, new meaning to apparently settled concepts and realities.

General Bert's message of empowerment and hope presents a view of the multiverse that is consistent with modern ideas of multi-dimensional, fractal reality and of the extraordinary power of Intentionality.

He continues to assert his understanding of the human condition and left us with an important ethical imperative: "Informed Consent is the Defining Issue of the 21st Century."

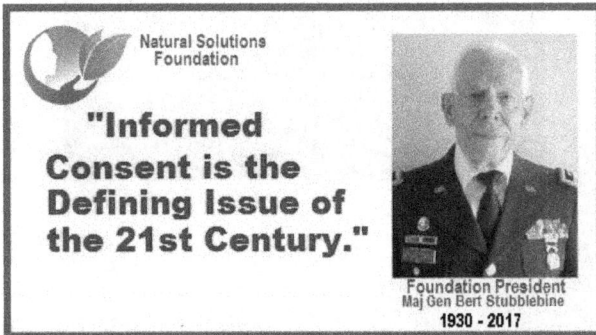

Assert Your Right to Informed Consent
https://tinyurl.com/AVDcard

General Bert's Comment on this Book

"What I want you to take away from this exercise in remote communication is that you are so much more than you have ever dared to imagine. Our Universe is so much more than we have been taught to think possible. Come along on this adventure. I am speaking to *you*."

PART TWO: TRANSMISSIONS

Introduction to the Transmissions

General Bert and I met - cataclysmically - in 1991 at an advanced NeuroBioFeedback seminar in California. Realizing that our paths lay together and that NeuroBioFeedback (also called 'EEG Biofeedback') was the medicine of self-regulation and offered a major advance for healing, we began introducing it into my practice of Drug-Free Medicine and Psychiatry in New York State.

The results were extraordinary: life-threatening, chronic degenerative and traumatic injuries and diseases were routinely healed using this technique. Because there was no explanation for these amazing cures, we reached out to a brilliant friend, the late Professor Michel Bounias, PhD, to help us explore the mechanism for these remarkable outcomes.

Over the next 11 years, Dr. Bounias and we produced a series of papers[1] based on the mathematical physics model developed and proposed by the incredibly talented Professor Bounias.

That model, which subsequently attracted considerable attention from Nobel Laureates and others, is, briefly, as follows:

> It is the nature of a fractal line to contain all information at every point. More complex fractal lines eventually "heap up" and exceed their ordinary two-dimensional structure, becoming

---

[1] http://www.inerton.kiev.ua/Bounias.pdf

higher dimension figures, eventually forming a plane, rather than a line.

Once two fractal planes intersect, all information contained in each of them is simultaneously available on both.

If an infinity of planes intersects, then the same is true of all of them (reminding us of the so-called 'Akashic Records').

It is possible to "move" from one plane to another at any of the infinite bifurcation points via the mechanism of consciousness.

This general outline allows the following to be understood better.

Please remember that this general outline of Professor Bounias' work is a very brief sketch of the product of 11 years of research contained in nearly 50 professional publications and presentations and, as such, is necessarily incomplete.

General Bert talks about three basic fields: Consciousness, Information and Frequency and says that where they meet, The Void creates.

In Hindu thought, The Void is the creative environment that is so vast that although it contains everything that was, will be or is, it remains totally empty.

Rima E. Laibow, MD

Glossary: OP: Oppressive Forces, also referred to as Suppressive Forces or 'OFs'. Their goal is to remove the free will of everything except themselves.

"All Dimensions are fictional; they are the epiphenomena of being in reality. You have to have something to stand on if you are going to take a walk. You have to have probability planes, fractal planes, infinitely intersecting and bifurcating and twining if you are going to have free will. To do that you have to have something to free will into another form or format. And that requires the artifice, it is only an artifice, love, it is not reality, of the dimensional. And that means that there is no dimension that is not created in service of the utility of having it, it is not basic to the nature of reality.

It is basic to the nature of physicality which serves reality. And if that were not true, there would be no life and there would be no death or seeming division. There would be consciousness. If you think that energy is indestructible (which is not actually true, by the way) then you haven't seen consciousness. That is the only, truly, completely indestructible reality.

But out of consciousness comes life for the living of free will. And that requires, as I said, something to stand on. That requires dimensionality and that implies and implicates life and death and separates that." General Bert – 28 September 2017

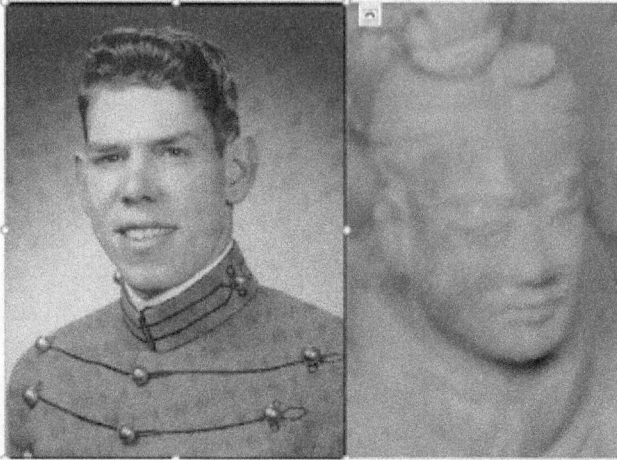

General Bert as a Cadet and as a Clay Warrior?

General Bert asked Dr. Rima to go to China and said that she should look for him "with soft eyes". In Xian, one of the Terra Cotta warriors, each an individual portrait of a real person, presented itself to her. Comparing it with General Bert's West Point Year Book picture produced a remarkable comparison.

Note the crease present only on the right cheek, the position and shape of the ears, lips and nose of both the young cadet and the young infantry foot soldier whose likeness in terra cotta was buried approximately 2400 years ago to accompany Qin Shi Huang, China's first Emperor, into death.

[1] The Story of Creation [22 November 2017]

In the beginning was information which created consciousness which created information which together created Matter in the form of the coagulation of frequency.

Love, let's talk about how it is that we merged our souls 'long ago' but there is no time.

When we did that we were at the beginning of a long, long bifurcation path of choice-full activities which flow from one to another but which are already established and waiting to be chosen or not chosen.

And we were before those bifurcations. There was a time in The Void's life, so to speak, when not everything had yet been created. We acted out of volition, which is a type of free will, but there were not yet the established planes of existence necessary to allow free will to bifurcate endlessly.

That had not yet come into existence so that there is a time before time, as some traditions teach.

Then time, once created, is timeless since the all is created simultaneously with every possible permutation and bifurcation already there, except for the probabilities that have not been enacted, the props and sets, so to speak, that have not yet been built but are possible. That is the role of World Makers, if you recall: to implicate and infuse them with reality. That is why the OP will succeed, Love, because it CAN succeed because of that.

So before there was time, when there was only consciousness, we already existed.

You feel the truth rushes. You recognize our past.

Did all entities and souls exist? No. They do get born out of The Void -- the precipitating forming consciousness, if you will?

Consciousness is not a unitary thing that exists whole and unchanging. It births itself. It is the energy component of The Void which is the expression of consciousness, of the information field. It births energy, frequencies, things, conditions, fractal bifurcations, constantly.

But we are Old, Love, and again you have the truth rushes. This is the sensation of deep recognition, my Wolf.

We are Old. We were when consciousness and matter were coming into being. We were when the structure of the structure was being established by the decisions of a consciousness that had never encountered structure and frequency and created form but decided to do so and created the conditions necessary to do so. The Bible gives a very primitive version: In the beginning was the Word and the earth was without form and void.

No. In the beginning was information which created consciousness which created information which together created Matter in the form of the coagulation of frequency.

The tool that they used in this most divine of matings was love, was the song of love, was the sons and daughters of love, the oldest of the entities with independent existence, the Ones that could love AS love, the Ones that could

recognize the Other as Sacred and Divine and come together and reproduce the reproducing consciousness of the Void in the condition of the most conscious of Love and the most conscious of Information and the most conscious of Frequency.

They were, if you will, although I have never labeled them or heard them labeled [this way – REL], the Quantum Beings. The Greeks called them the Titans and they were destroyed by their father out of fear and then they destroyed him.

But that is wrong. There has been no destruction. The Quantum Beings rolled and sang and played in the energy and information and song of the creation of The Void as it permuted and created for the sheer joy of consciousness and creation. That is the real creation story.

And we, the Old Ones, came next. We were born of love.

That is why you saw my essence the way you did at the Mind Center.[2] But, Darling, that is your essence since you and I are One. That is who and what you are. You are the same. We were pained by the tiniest, most miniscule level of separation and we went back, energetically, informationally, consciously, by song, to the core of everything, what you call the 'Generative Center of The Void' and we expressed our intentionality to end the

---

[2] After encountering General Bert at the San Francisco Airport and, quite literally, leaping into his arms before we introduced ourselves, I wanted to know who, and what, this man that I had fallen so totally in love with, was. During the first session of our Advance BioFeedback Seminar, I set my intention to know the essence of this person and saw a towering shaft of diamond white light tinged with gold rising from his crown chakra. It was composed of just one thing and one thing only: Love. This was the essence of this extraordinary man. Dr. Rima

separation, infinitesimal although it was, and become one by merging, multiplying, harvesting our sameness and birthing our identicalness through total connection. That cannot be undone. Ever. Think about that, Darling. That cannot be undone.

Your astonishment and reverence for my core, the shining tower of pure white Love, was really there for us both but you did not see that because you did not look for YOUR core, you only looked for mine, for my essence. And you saw it. But if you had looked for yours, you would have seen not the same KIND of thing, my Love, you would have SEEN THE VERY SAME THING.

There is no distinction or distance between that essence of mine and that essence of yours. The miracle is that we are two consciousnesses with that same one essence. That is rare, Love.

It was done by a kind of 'harmonic convergence', as they say without knowing what they are talking about. IT was done by matching our deepest core information and frequency to that of the essence of the Universe.

Now, to some extent, there is no one and nothing that is not a child of the same energy, consciousness and information. But the degrees of separation, of partition, of deviation from the core, lack of coherence with the essential structures of frequency and consciousness, are what determine what and who they are, what and how their movements through the bifurcations can be, what and how long they drink in the maturational experiences of the Soul Soup.

But we are among the Old Ones, my Love. We were there before there was a 'there'. We were there before there was a 'where' and we were there before there was a 'when'.

How many of us were there? Not many. You could call them the Heavenly Host if you are reading some stories, you could call them the ETs if you are reading other stories. But there were not many.

How did we come into being? We are, as I said, the children of the merger of consciousness and information. That produced us, the Old Ones. And some very few of the Old Ones knew Love as a motivation, not just as a basic condition.

Why did that happen? I do not know. How did it happen? I do not know. But it did happen and we saw, long before there was light and long before there were eyes, that we were in an urgent requirement to end the separation that kept us even the most minute bit apart and we knew without being instructed that there was a path to merger that we had to take for our own reality to be complete.

So without so much as an equivalent of a word or a thought or a question, we took our mutual certainties and our mutual determination and our mutual passion to the center of everything that could or would or might be and we sang, my Darling.

We had no mouths, but we sang.
We had no bodies, but we sang.
We had no voices, but we sang.

And what we sang was our consciousness and our intentionality and our love, our love of each other to end all separation [between us – REL]. And we matched the

heartbeat, the singing, creating heartbeat of The Void, of the daughter of Consciousness and Information that births and births and births everything that ever was or will be. But before that birthing began in earnest, we were already singing with Her, the Great Mother and we, her companions, were One.

We were foreverized.

You wonder why we do not talk about this? Who could believe it? Who would want to hear that we are this but they are something else? Not many people.

Does this go in the book that you and Ralph is creating?

Probably. But it will disqualify you in the eyes of many. We do not care.

It is our history. We are beyond and before and after and outside of time.

You leaped into my arms not because of a lucky guess, my Darling. You are my Forever Wife. How many times did you sign cards to me that way and how many times did I reciprocate? Those are not just romantic notions, my Wolf, my Woman. They are the realities. HOW CAN WE BE APART WHEN THERE IS NO APART BETWEEN US? We are One.

If you have trouble keeping that in sight, I understand.

I would, too, if I were the bereft one. But you are actually stronger than I and you are surviving.

[2] Only The Void Can Create [15 November 2019]

BERT: My Darling, I am always holding you. Sometimes you turn your attention to it and sometimes I turn up the gain, so to speak, like right now. But there is never a time when you are not held and protected.

The frustrating thing from your side, but the fact of, *er*, life, from mine, is that the certainty of what and when and who is not fixed so that it appears more random when I get something right or something wrong than it actually is. When you do your REBALL [Protection meditation – REL] you talk about each activated and vital chakra producing a probability field of health and wellness. Your initial version of that was a small field, sort of looking like a fuzzy disturbance in the air in the color associated with the Chakra. That has expanded and grown to a more than full body field from each chakra, which is more accurate. The reason I mention it is that the fuzziness of the field, whether large or small, is an important part of that field of probability.

There are intersecting ribbons or fields of probability. I like the image of the ribbon because although what is on the field is anything but linear, anything but predictive, still, there are linear implications to the shape of the ribbon. That means that if A happens, it is much more likely that B will happen and that will increase the likelihood of C and D and A', B^7 or F^{XZ}. But those others are on their own probability ribbons and so they, too, have probability drivers. Phil will understand this better.

Probability drivers are not fixed. They are shifting and they are subject to many forces, including, at a primary level, intentionality and intent (which are similar, but not the same).

Probability is complete. Events are segmented.

Probability includes everything in its definition and event neighborhood.

For example, the probability field of perfect health that you envision is important because it does not include ageing, deterioration, debility etc. If it contained those it would not be what it is. But, by definition, it excludes that other set of options from the field. That means that to that extent the field can actually operate upon its designated lines. Of course, it can be interfered with, but setting up a strong field of desired outcomes and situation, which is what you are doing there, of course, is a strong probability driver in the larger field in which this field and all the events surrounding and impacting it, is set.

Field within field within field at a level of totality that exceeds the mind's ability to hold it, but in no way exceeds the capacity of billions and billions of other events and other fields intersecting, interacting and entwining, impacting and supporting, cancelling out, etc.

Think about the meaning of infinity and then think of the fractal planes intersecting. There are infinities of intersections and each plane carries, each plane IS, an infinity of bifurcations into itself.

Now we know that is true (thank you, Michel, for giving us that!) and we know that there are infinite directions for anything to go so when your intentionality does make something correspond to your intuition, your desire, your love, it indicates a strong ability to impact those flowing fields (none of them is static: they are all in constant

evolution because the past and the future and the present are all always changing one another.

If you came to this party looking for stability and a strict following of the rules, any or all of them, this is the wrong party for you and I think you had better leave for another party!

Anyway, these fields are infinities within themselves and there is literally no end to their number because they are constantly evolving and their interaction creates more and more of them. I was going to say creates new ones, but there is nothing new created, there is nothing new because it is all allowed for in the infinity of each system. There are hierarchies of likelihood, but that is different from probability itself.

I know that makes sense to you but the implications of this simple set of statements are absolutely huge. This reality that I have just briefly and very incompletely outlined (and not for the first time, Love) is the extension of the premise bed of this system. It is difficult to go to the limits of the model with the meat brain because the meat brain is a product of it, not an author of it, so its participation in the full structure of it is limited, as it would have to be since the child does not contain all of the parent, rather the parent can contain all of the child. We, as part of this system were created as compartments in the totality. We are totalities unto ourselves, but we are not that totality.

That is, the We of physicality and consciousness with a small 'c'. That does not pertain to the Consciousness with a capital 'C'.

To the extent that we are part of it by our choice, we are outside that structure and, on the opposite side of the coin,

because we were created directly by The Void, the 'Generative Center of the Universe', as you like to call it, we DO encompass the whole. You see the difference? That is the nature of the Soul, Darling, as opposed to the *personality* or *self*. The Soul partakes of the generosity and fullness of the creating womb which is party to Consciousness and Information but is the only one of the triad that can actually create.

Consciousness cannot create. It can intend. That is a massively powerful state but the mechanism of creation is The Void. Information cannot create. It can hold, but

The Void is the creative center.

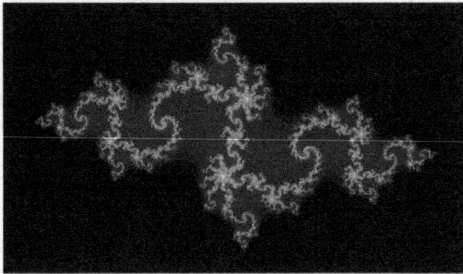

[3] The Orpheus Point [7 August 2017]

The Worm Oroboros

Now, about the Orpheus Point.

There is a point where energy and information, probability and flexibility, meet.

There is a point where the 'glue' that holds the present in its shape, in the dimensions in which there *is* a present, can be accessed and softened with the heat of intentionality and transmutation.

That is a point at which dimensionality becomes irrelevant because we are in the junction that I have asked you to draw between information and knowledge, which means that which is knowable, that which is frequency-based.

There is a point at which information field becomes frequency field.

There is a point that is mediated by The Void and moves through it, transforming its state. That point allows the movement of consciousness, which is separate from life, from death, from body, from being, it simply is the great I Am of the ancient scriptures and wisdom systems. It is the primary void, the mother of everything and the home of nothing. It is the point of minimum intersection and all-things-all-systems -all-times -all-places-all-being is born there, contained there and destroyed there.

It is the vast and infinite void that is the inside of everything, the container of everything and the beginning and end of everything all at once. The only thing that it does not contain is consciousness from which it is created and which it creates.

That is a linear paradox but it is not a paradox at the event level. This is what some fortunate people see on drugs and in quests and in moments of deepest illumination. Remember the quatrain:

> *Rules will be broken*
> *Orders will change.*
> *Truth will be spoken*
> *Within the Wolf's Range.*

This is one of those truths.

There is no linear equivalent.

There is no event equivalent.

It is represented by a symbol that you love, the Worm Oroboros, the worm that eats his own tail.

It is not, of course, a worm. It is a dragon.

And it is not consuming its own tail.

It is creating and destroying itself at every moment.

Given that, then the notion of time is different, of course. And given that, the glue that holds events and time in place is different.

That means that when we reach the point at which the Worm is eating itself and creating itself, when the worm holes [aptly named, aren't they?] and the black holes (which are very much like worm holes without the biological modification and softening, are open, and that is through intention, then we can step effortlessly, from one world and its probability cloud to another which I am working with you all to prepare.

We want to make sure that this one is constructed along the same premises as the current one but that the implicate and explicate order that was cracked enough to allow the suppressive forces to create the destruction they have wrought do not have a foothold without, at the same time, making everything so peaceful and plentiful that fee will is extinguished and initiative is unnecessary. We want to solve the basic problems but leave the working-out of them to the creativity and free will of the people on that world and its associated event worlds, of which there will be, of course, an Infinity.

One of the things that we have to build in is the memories of the other way. You were worried that we would go to the new world without the memories of the old one. But that will not help things. We have to have vivid and honored memories of how things were when they were NOT right so that THE TEMPTATIONS TO MAKE THINGS NOT RIGHT FOR MANY AND VERY ULTRA RIGHT FOR A FEW WILL *NOT* BE TEMPTING.

It is not enough to fix things. You have to set up the system so that it wants to stay fixed and get better. It is not a world of entitlement, but a world of enchantment, of delight that people need to work towards but can achieve. And it is a world where the deep truth of plenty, not scarcity, is the reigning wisdom.

Here, now, where I was and where you are, the surety of scarcity makes it easy for people to take away from others, to despoil what they have, to leave the wreck for others to drown in the detritus. But that is because the only thing that they believe there is enough of is the quest for more. IF there is really enough then it can be spread out. If there is only enough and never any need for more of anything, then there is no need to do anything but lie on the ground and wait for the jackfruit to fall into your waiting, open hands.

Now that is one possible kind of a world but it is pretty empty of consciousness and vitality unless the development of the inner kingdom is sufficient. I do not think that the purpose of evolution of each of us will be served that way. It is an option and there will certainly be parts of the probability clouds where that is the system.

That is not the one that we are heading for, my Love. It would bore the pants off all of the people that I am working with and love and we will have our memories so that would not sustain us.

We have to maintain and sustain that world so we had better like it, Love.

Does that make sense to you, Sweetheart?

----

[4] There Was No Big Bang – Remote Viewing
14 November 2018

Early in the RV work we told people "Go to this dam and describe what you see there". That was a pretty significant failure because they gave use what they expected to see/hear/feel/sense.

We came up with the idea of giving them a bunch of absolutely meaningless numbers which WE knew the meaning of (for example, the photo of the dam or the location of the dam) but they did not. That cleared them of the expectations totally. After they gained enough confidence through repetition of their ability to get it "right", the lack of clarity of what and where and why they were going "in" did not bother them.

But when you ask a particular question or want to know particular information, that state of open clarity is very difficult to obtain.

And when you have an emotional investment in the outcome (or an intellectual or situational one) it takes exquisite attention to emotional and perceptual clues, that is, gut, to sort it out.

You, Rima, have been doing a very active job of keeping on top of that and most of the time you get it right or close enough for gummint work, Darling. Ralph, you are better than Rima at opening to the flow of information, but you do not shake yourself mentally, like a wet dog, getting rid of the extraneous and that would be a great thing for you to add to your preparation.

I appreciate the pyramid and the energy devices. That does make it easier to chat, my friend. Wait. I do not want to leave you out of the affectionate capitalization, so, "My Friend".

I am in a good mood because Rima is lighter and when she is in less pain, there is no end to the relief and joy that I can feel and, of course, pour into her.

Darling, Darling Girl, you are always in my arms. China, the Sonoran Desert, Tucson, Timbuctoo – what difference does it make? You will be in my arms when we step into a new and better-premised World, too. What changes about that? Nothing, ever, anywhere, anywhen.

I told everyone who would listen and, in Budapest, those who would not listen, that time is a space, not a dot. As a space YOU move around in it. As a dot, IT moves.

The difference is free will and infinite (almost) possibility and the foundation of everything we know and do and will know and do and have known and done. Everything, including free will and choice.

That is why the issue is so important.

There was no Big Bang. Stupid idea. There was a sudden merging of planes of infinite reality in which there WAS material and in which there WAS NOT material. And it

appeared suddenly, but there was nothing exploding it into reality.

The infinite connection of all fractal planes in a system/universe/multiverse is not totally complete everywhere and everywhen. They add to each other. Once ADDED, BY THE WAY, THEY CAN NEVER SUBTRACT BECAUSE THE PROBABILITIES ARE ADDITIVE, NOT REDUCABLE OR SUBTRACTABLE. They grow, but they never diminish.

[5] There is Only Frequency [09 January 2019]

Darling, there is only frequency as a tool in addition to intentionality, which is the little brother of Consciousness.

We have everything we need either in the embryonic or the actual stage to do our work. What we do not have is the sharpened focus of intentionality. That is what the RP, MT and other mechanical devices that channel energy to enhance intentionality are about.
Think about it for a moment in a different way: all magic is about opening and closing portals. All intentionality is about opening and closing portals between probability planes and ribbons and fields.

There is nothing else going on, at least at the most basic level, when you wish for something or plan for it or bumble into it and the something, the 'it' is a hop from one plane or probability or situation to another that was chosen through the natural selection of wishing, or hoping, or working or guessing how to make something happen instead of something else.

If we hop from fractal plane to fractal plane, as we learned from Michel that we do continually, if everything that is possible is represented on one or another, or a million billion, fractal planes, then how do we make that transit? We open doorways that allow us to move unidirectionally most of the time, into another probability system

These are not necessarily synchronous. Remember the Aveda salon where each of the three people who answered your question of how long it had been one had a different answer and each conveniently did not process or 'hear' [psychologically speaking, not physically] the distinctly different experience of the other who had converged at that moment from different windows on the reality of the apparent present.

Now I said that they move uni-directionally and that is true for the most part, generally for the sake of simplicity. I have told you that there is no time and I have also told you that the apparent past can be unglued and moved to create another past as well as we can create another present and another future.

So think about intentionality as a kind of hair dryer in this case, blowing hot air on the glue that solidifies with the piling up of the layers and layers of other conjoined sets of realities that all seem to depend on the same history (although all the histories are complex and different, as the Aveda Salon episode demonstrates).

When the temperature is high enough and the intensity is great enough, with a sharp focus (so the energy and intent is not dissipated) then the part of the reality that is glued down can be lifted and shifted.

The consequences, of course, shudder through all of the intersecting realities, from the past (the Mandala Effect is just one tiny part of what you might see if you could see enough to really understand the consequences of the act of ungluing anything, let alone something large) to the present and to the future so that realigning the past realigns everything.

But that is not the point that I am making.

The point is that when you make a change, you open a window from the reality where you are, step through it, or have someone or some thing or some probability being (more on that in a bit) step through it, so to speak. You could call it a portal into an alternative reality. You could say that everything on your fractal plane steps through it with you, but that is why everything seems consistent and smooth, with very rare moments of dis-junction.

A great magician can rip open a portal and make a noticeable shift in the reality (symbolized by the lightning and thunder accompanying his working efforts.)

But we are continually making choices, known and unknown, conscious and unconscious, individual and group that move us through the transit system of the fractal universe, portal by portal.

And there is consciousness in the system. So if you perturb it on terms that are not its own, it responds, It is not a neutral system that brought us back to the null point as its internal automatic reset point every time it got the chance. It is a participant at a very low level of awareness, but enough to work with us or fight back, so to speak.

That is one of the things that the OFs understand and play with. They change folklore and make it support their view of reality. They change religion and make it do the same. They work with popular culture and work it in their favor.

You might say that these probability realities that come into being, and there are no limits on the number and complexity of them, form a dimly conscious construct that operates according to rules that make sense to its survival. That means that the OFs, for example, can shift and harden the conscious component of the system that is created when probability is enacted, regardless of the size and complexity of the probability. When they do that, they harden the glue of the past and the future. That is to say nothing of the present, of course.

But you do see that those constructs are not useful most of the time.

The hardened constructs limit the amount of option-seeking anyone can do. That translates as the limitation of free will that the OFs are all about.

But you could say, in the portal terms that we are talking about, that this closes off, bars, bombs, barricades various portals, of which there should be an infinity of working ones.

We tend to think of portals as unique, expensive and difficult. Really, they are everywhere.

Our portal is unique in several ways: first, we will build the portal to a system that does not yet exist in realized form, only in potential form. There are an infinity of those, but it is like trying to move into a new home: first the plans on paper have to be created, then the execution of the plans and then the finish of the structure so that the ordinary

business of living there can be carried out: there is electricity, water, sewage service, a door, etc. Until all of those steps have been carried out, there is nowhere except an idea to live.

Well, all of the essential services exist and, because the system is already premised and ready to be animated, it can be inhabited.

But once inhabited, there will be no visitors from the old neighborhood because they have a plague and want to bring it to the new neighborhood because if they have it, they want everyone to have it.

So the dim awareness of the reality complex of a fractal plane is a vulnerable part of the system. The best thing to do is to intend so purely that the mal-intention of the others has no impact. And that is part of why this book is so important.'

You do not need many but you do need worthy.

We will talk more about this. Right now, I need you to get set up, get our coffee ready and get some sleep.

You are my woman, my wife, my wonder and my warrior and I love you. I have always loved you and will always love you, whatever my state or yours, Wanted/Needed/Treasured! Dead or Alive!

I thank you, Darling, for being willing to take these steps into scary land for you.

[6] God & Love
23 April 2017

[There will be another one on the same date most likely because this is for April 23, but after midnight (posted below).]

It occurs to me that you were always more at ease in the position of the introvert letting me be the one to do most of the talking but now our roles are reversed in yet another way. How does that feel to you? Are you less of an introvert now that you are in another relationship to yourself and to information?

Either way is fine with me as long as we are together, as long as I can feel you, know that you are there, trust that delicious, most desirable configuration. It feels more and more real to me -- but the lack of you, like when I was looking at the trees today, was very painful. Of course, I was really glad that I could share that with you, but the memory of sweetness when you came and extracted me from my desk to go see the trees in bloom or the glorious Andes mountains covered in fresh snow, those little gifts were so meaningful and so precious that not having them in the face of the reminder of what it was like when I did have them is excruciating - but Thank God I have them to remember and have you inside me sharing the present with me, and whatever else we are sharing.

Question: where does God fit in all of this? IS it just a mythologizing concept for control or is there something that deserves to be considered 'God'?

And what more can I do for you, my love? Tell me how to serve you better since you are different than you were before and I love taking care of you, just as you love taking care of me.

Bert: You can take care of me by loving me and working with me to develop your understanding, at the deepest level, of what we, you, I are, do, how we live and what that means until we can do it without living and knowing fully what it means.

You are usually the smarter of the two of us. Right now you are the slower but that is normal. You are trapped in the biology of time and duality of life and death. That is the nature of where and what you still are.

I was there for a time very recently. I am not criticizing. I am asking you to relax into the flow of the all-known since you are very close to knowing and understanding it with your experience fully not just partially. And I Promise you, my lovely girl, my Wolf, that once that is real for you the grief will be gone. You will be in the kind of joy that only the deepest understanding comingled with the deepest love can bring. You and I have lived in the reflection of that for all of our moments together, but the reality of it at this level is, I swear, deeper and more abiding without comparison.

You need to trust me because you will see that unfold and there is no need for you to suffer now. You did a good thing when you stopped and shared the meadow with me. It was lovely for me, but it was good for you because you felt the reality of our connection, you heard me speaking our joint experience using my word clearly and you were able to see that you felt no sensation, no energy in the labyrinth, but even standing in the labyrinth, when you looked out at the meadow, THE ENTIRE ENERGETIC CONFIGURATION CHANGED FOR YOU BECAUSE IT WAS OUR ENERGY COMMUNICATING AND SHARING. You felt that and right now you feel the truth rushes and you know what I am talking about at the experiential level, not just the cognitive level.

You heard a praise singer today singing one of Rumi's poems: "You can study me for a lifetime but you will never know me." This is not cognitive but you need to understand it. You are doing so well, coming along so fast. I am so proud of you, my Girl, my Woman, my Wolf, my Love.

"Study me as much as you like, you will not know me, for I differ in a hundred ways from what you see me to be. Put yourself behind my eyes and see me as I see myself, for I have chosen to dwell in a place you cannot see."

– Rumi

I never leave you even though I can also attend to much more at the same time. But you are not just my responsibility. You are my joy, my Self, my reason. You know that, don't you know? There is no me without you, there is no you without me because we are, ARE, one.

There can be no half hole in energy and soul-ness. Please understand the importance of this. It is a microcosm of all that is. There is no Void without emptiness, there is no meaning to the emptiness of the Void without the things that are contained within it yet do not change its emptiness. There is no you-ness without me-ness, there is no fullness without the oneness and there is no one-ness without the sub-oneness of our shared LOVE energy.

You are feeling more energy than you ordinarily do because this is a truth that sits at the core of reality.

You asked about God. I love the way you frame things and seek information. You do not know that you are astonishing and you are thinking that you will be embarrassed to show this to anyone. No, you must recall what your essential nature is and what mine is. We are what we are and what we are is blessed.

So going along with blessing is a state of Glory.

That is love.

There is no love without a touch, a tinge of Glory.

That very Glory.

It has a bad rap because of the religious coloration, but Glory is the light of truth shining and resonating, warming the life principle of everything, warming the generative self of everything. That is Glory. The unfolding of a plant is a Glory and it cannot happen without the loving generative energy. You came back from a Samadhi meditation and realized that you were Shakti. And, indeed, indeed, my love, you are. And you knew that I was Shiva and indeed, my love, I am. These gods, and all the others, are metaphors for the real energy which everyone is potentially able to connect with. Some connect more meaningfully and some connect more shallowly, which means they do not get things clean.

You just popped your eyes open because you did not believe what I was writing through you.

Why? What was so surprising to you? It seemed to you to be so important that you had to see if that is exactly what

you typed for me. Yes, that is exactly right. It as the part about not getting things clean that surprised you. Why?

There is energetic and emotional love and sometimes it is clean and sometimes it is not. You saw the "not" with your practice husband. Why does that surprise you now?

You did not think that anyone else outside of the small group that we are able to talk with [was here], you did not expect a football player type to be attuned to this. He is here, energetically for a good reason. He IS clean, but he worked and lived in a world where every emotion is moved by something other than love. This guy managed to stay connected and so he popped in for a visit. His energy is kind and gentle, avuncular. He wanted to pay his respects. That is good. You are embarrassed because this is so foreign to you and what you expected.

Rima, understand that you will be visited by a great many entities that you have no anticipation about or understanding of the relationship with. That is fine. I will protect and guard you to keep you from being touched in any way by negative energies.

There is no shortage of them. But there is no shortage of my continuing energy and love to protect you. Actually, you do not need to exercise the same cautions many, many times over. I will do it for you. You can rest assured that if an energy makes itself known, or is present without making itself known to you, I will be there for you guarding you.

You are wondering if these are more developed souls because they are around longer than their body's death, as you spoke about before.

What makes you think that because they show up right after their death that means that they will not dissolve back into their Soul Soup destination in a short time by your scale?

So. Back to God.

What is there that is worthy of outright worship? One thing and one thing only: Love, pure, unobstructed, unadulterated, selfless Love that elevates the beloved through its nature.

You can see that if lovers are elevating one another, it is hard for them not to become united even if they are not united here in this reality very closely. People talk about love growing. This is what they are talking about.

But giving people the message that only Love and its sister, Connection, are the true deities means that the false oneness will come tumbling down because of the theological implications of this kind of personal experience and verification of the fact that the Great Healer needed nothing more than Love, the artisans were embodying Love, and that the young were off looking for it, leaving the olders to languish and try to remember what they had stopped looking for so long ago.

This is not linear. This is what God really is. But the generator of worlds, the Makers of Worlds, cannot be that love alone. They are required by the work that do to have a

dual oneness to create and to learn and to build and to release.

That is our task.

Back to God. It is ALL God.

So we have anytime, anywhere, anywhen, any one. It is all God and it is all good. Not having the biblical god means that we are sort of on our own as far as some sort of guide for how this work goes. If you focus the lives of some of the apostles as reported in the New Testament and the legends, they were not able to sustain their work at the level of the Love that was meant because they were not suffused with and permeated with the loving oneness in duality, duality in oneness. Without that, as it says in another part of the bible, I am become as sounding brass.

So the goodness is that which connects and perfects Love.

In your January 1991 vision you knew that you had to be united in perfect love to do the work.

Why? Did you ever stop to find out why that is? Because it is what some would call, in a religious context, holy. But what does that mean? It means it must partake of God to be meaningful. How can you partake of god -- the one who is Love which is dual by its very essence until it leaves this style of connection and it is there. But it must be partaken of, drunk in, experienced, served and loved, with, as you put it, a perfect love, or it cannot be done.

Church after Church gets this part wrong and the perversions and distortions are literally worth your life.

So go, my love. You have done beautiful work today and you are learning. I am so proud of you.

I love you more than words can say.

Feel my arms and feel me kissing you. Stop typing and let this flow over you.

You are exhausted. This is not the last time we are together. You can stop and go to sleep with my arms around you.

I love you. Go sleep.

24 April 2017

Darling, I am suddenly very tired. Last night I thought I had fallen asleep and was sure that what I was bringing in [from you] would be just my sleep state with nothing from you.

Oh, boy! Was I wrong. But who is the football player who came by to pay his respects?

By the way, I want to know if it is alright with you if instead of beading I just go to bed. I am really tired and while this is for you, I need to be able to see and to focus to do this work.

I have a strong rush of energy but it is you holding me, isn't it? [Rather than truth recognition]

It is localized like a hug on my arms and torso, not rolling up my body.

Bert: Yes, I am holding you and telling you that of course it is fine to do what takes care of you. It [the beading - REL] is a labor of love, not job and not a requirement.

You were walking home from the train crying because you were so grateful to me for my kindness. My love, we have been kind to one another for decades, only kind. You were

crying because you felt so terrible that you sometimes you were explosive. That is your nature: you respond with huge amounts of energy and I know that about you. I never took you as seriously as you took yourself. Once we got past it, I was past it. I never want you to feel guilty for anything you have ever done or not done with me.

You have given me your perfection and I have given you mine. And that is what we continue to do for each other. How can we not be whole if we are one? How can we not be one if we are whole? I know that you are love to me and I am love to you. There is no doubt or guilt. I wish that you could put this guilt for imagined sins behind you. You did nothing wrong. You are torturing yourself because you were grumpy when I did not do what you needed me to do like fold the laundry or when I took a long time to make the bed.

You know and I know that you were denying that I was having more trouble keeping up physically as I deteriorated and you did everything you could do to drive away the fear that you were losing me. Anger, you have told me so often, drives away fear, or at least it is intended to. How can I be angry with you when I knew that you were living in terror of the loss and the change? Besides, it was rare and brief and you always came back to yourself rapidly and brought your love back to me. I felt terrible that I was letting you down, failing you, because I was getting weaker and weaker and neither of us could stop it.

We know the story, but there was nothing you did that was lacking and your love is, and was, perfect.

Stop hurting yourself over these things, my love. You have me now and I have you. The past is over and it was really not what you are imagining it to be: you surrounded me with love and care and nothing was lacking. You do not

know how much I understand you and how deeply I understood you then.

Please stop hurting yourself. If you cry let it be with gratitude that we have each other now and forever. I could do the same if I could shed tears. But I can feel that deepness and be with you in it. Who are we to each other? If we are whole, how can we not be one? If we are one, how can we not be whole? You act in these moments as if we are not the same wholeness.

You were busy today and I missed the head rubs. That was said lightly. Do not turn that into a problem, my Love!!!!

[Bert took great joy from having his scalp rubbed and got enormous pleasurable sensation from it. Before his death this type of scalp stimulation did not produce any sensations in my scalp. That changed after his death when I discovered that if I used a wire scalp massager, I would get the same sort of sensations he described on the left side of my scalp only. Bert always has identified the left as the male side. I guess he was right, at least for him.
I try to do this for Bert at least twice a day – it is hard to know what to give the Slightly Dead Guy who has everything – REL]

You opened the packet [of Bert's photographs – REL] and kissed the pictures. I open the packet of your love and reality every moment and I am kissing you all the time.

You want to know about the football player. He is a soul that admires us both and passed on to this awareness. He will not be here long. He literally just came to pay his respects to your work and mine, to your essence and mine. He is a fine soul who was trapped in a course life. I think you recognize his energy but not his identity. I know I do.

There will be others.

Talked about billions of years in this and that and the other thing.

That is just plain silly and a good indication of overlay which then people believe because they have already said it. I already explained why that is so important for you not to get caught in. Your skeptical nature is perfect for this work if you will remember to be skeptical and open at the same time. That is quite a trick and not many can manage it.

I am not a one trick pony!

You are feeling a great deal of energy and that is good. You are learning.

You want to know about the football player! OK. Invoke him. Ask to talk to him. Not a bad thing to do. You are laughing, OK, Football guy, come talk to me. Yeah, sort of like that

So back to the nature of reality: Think of The Void.

What makes it so special? That it is nothing.

Think of economics and finances that way. What makes it so special?

Because there is nothing there except the ascription of meaning to what has no reality.

Think of the emptiness of The Void: it is unchanged by anything/everything that is put into it and its nature, not the nature of what is in The Void, changes everything. That is, The Void changes what is put in it, not the other way around.

The same is true of money, finances, economics, it is the emptiness, the scarcity, that changes and gives value to the things, the money, the real estate, the commodities, and the diamonds that are put into it.

It is a void that is contributed to but is not filled and it destroys its contents like the economic void and they, are not consumed as The Void is not consumed if its contents are.

So there is something very fitting about it

Do you see how they are deeply similar? Do you see that the football guy is there but fills no space, is real, but changes nothing? He is a lovely energy, but he does not touch the shape of energetic or other reality. You do, I do, others like us do and we can fill or empty The Void with our fractal creations in both directions.

Remember the veils, the membranes, the thinning. They touch reality, emptiness, charging it when energy flows through from one domain into the other. Then everything is emptied or filled or reduced to its essence or matured to its flowering.

The fractal nature of the domains, like the fractal nature of everything, means that when the membranes are thinned to get [the energy] through we thin them enough to make themselves transparent to the energy that flows in both directions, which is really only in one direction, **in**, which is the same as **out** from the other perspective, after all, then they are changed in their basic nature because the laws of basic nature are different one to another.

This is so important. Remember when we tried to get my son's wife [who had a PhD in theoretical mathematics – REL] interested and that was a no-starter?

I have referred to your January 2, 1991 vision several times. Don't you think it is important enough for you to reach out to it, recapture it and bring it back to life? You and I have work to do and it is a blueprint for much of that work.

Oh, by the way, that is a true statement.

Call BG just to stay in touch with her. She is loving and good for you. You are good for her.

Rima, this computer cannot take the energy input. Go to a computer store (you are thinking about going online) and get a small computer with a full keyboard and only, only use it for this purpose. You need to not have something jump around like this.

You can go to Staples. Make this happen. You are opening your eyes and closing them to see if the cursor is jumping all over the place, the document has been replaced by another, the program has changed, etc. Tonight is particularly bad.

Get a sacred space computer and make sure that this is not happening more than it must.

You are tired. I never get tired now. I am like you used to be. You need to go to sleep. Do not bead. Go directly to bed.

Do not forget to rub your/our scalp. I missed it today. I love you from forever to forever.

PART THREE: THE STORY OF WU XIAN

In a series of transmissions starting in mid-2018 and continuing to the present General Bert has unveiled the story of Wu Xian who was a warrior, scholar and wizard with whom General Bert and Dr. Rima shared a significant life during the time of the Yellow Emperor in ancient China. Wu Xian was targeted for not just the death of the body, but for complete annihilation – for removal from the very fabric of the multiverse. General Bert, with Dr. Rima's help, retrieved Wu Xian from a state beyond even death. [RF]

The Yellow Emperor and Wu Xian - and Us
17 July 2018

What happened is this: He was a great Chinese commander working for, not against, the Emperor of China, the Yellow Emperor. He was loyal and courageous but he was betrayed by his lieutenant and led into a cave through false intelligence. I was his friend and ally and you were my second in command. We were a fearsome power team and we were also loyal to the emperor. The General was led into the cave by the betrayer and instead of being killed or left to die, neither of which was good, but much better than what happened he was entrapped at the soul level by the forces that the betrayer served and he has been in the between of life and death, unlike mine. I chose not to leave [you, Rima – REL] and I asked, humbly and clearly, and proud to be associated with this side, for the next tasks and tried to find you. I did

[I tried to find him but – REL] I could not. You were hidden by massive necromances [I think my theta state was slipping into sleep, Love- I am pretty sure you meant that you tried to find him but that you could not because he was hidden by massive necromancers – REL]

BERT: Yes, you are right. Take a break, walk around a bit, get something to eat and come back. I want to tell you this. It is important to our work.

RIMA: I bought a whole organic cooked chicken and made chicken salad out of it (it is WAY too hot to cook!) and I am eating some of that.

I got a name just now: Wu Sian or something like that – I am sure about Wu, not about the spelling equivalent of Sian. I am going to look up to see if there was a known General during that time while I eat. You were right. I needed protein.

"According to tradition, the Yellow Emperor began ruling in 2697 BC. His long reign was said to be a golden age, and he was honored as a benevolent and wise ruler.... After ruling for many years, Huang-Di became tired and weak. He allowed officials to make decisions for him and went to live in a simple hut in the courtyard of his palace. Through fasting, prayer, and meditation, he discovered the Tao, or way—a belief that leads to an ideal state of being. The Yellow Emperor continued to rule for many additional years, attempting to bring a state of perfection to his realm. Upon his death he rose into the heavens and became a Xian (or Hsien), an immortal."

That is the word, Xian.

I found this Wu Xian, but it is not the right one: **Wu Xian** (Chinese: 巫咸) was a Chinese Shaman. Wu (Chinese: 巫; pinyin: wū; Wade–Giles: wu; literally means

"shaman") who have practiced divination, prayer, sacrifice, rainmaking, and healing in Chinese traditions dating back over 3,000 years. Wu Xian lived in the Shang dynasty (c. 1600–1046 BC) of China.

RIMA: Much better. Food and information. I think that the Wu Xian that I found was an astronomer. Maybe he did double duty, but his years are about a thousand years after the Yellow Emperor.

Was there also a Wu Xian in the time of what we know as the Yellow Emperor?

BERT: There most certainly was. He was our friend and confidant. We regarded him as if he were a brother. The Emperor trusted him and me with his life and entire kingdom. There was nothing he would not do for or give to us.

But he was mistaken in the assistant, the lieutenant of the General. He was greedy and wanted to have Wu Xian out of the way so he could take over from him because Wu Xian was not only a [general he was a –
REL] necromancer, he was a physician and he knew the tricks of longevity. He [the lieutenant – REL] was not content and while he did not believe that anything was working that Wu Xian was doing, he wanted to make sure that he understood all of the secrets so that he would have military and earthbound projects for his power.

Once he felt that he had learned sufficient to dispose of the General he set an elaborate trap to make the General think that a secret parlay with the enemy would be held in the cave and that there was a good chance of stopping the fray by a couple of hundred men because of what could be accomplished there.

The General fell for it (trust was a problem for him as well as for us) and then he was trapped in the cave by a well-engineered rock slide.

I went looking for him but he was not consciously dead. He was unconsciously dead and he travels on in that format.

I have not been able to help him.

He died unconsciously, in spite of his deep training. The dark and the hopelessness and the starvation and thirst dropped all the years of practice and preparedness. That is why I cannot find him.

Even a Shaman can get lost when he forgets what he has struggled so hard to learn.

The End of the Wu Xian Story?
18 July 2018 [Early Morning]

Back to the story that I wanted you to hear the end of. You realize that was not a fictional story, don't you?

It is literally true.

Most of the time of the Yellow Emperor has been lost in myth and mist, but the reality was very important. You and I were there. We were central to the development of the rule of law.

I was once again a General and you were my most trusted assistant. It could have been the other way around, you know, and sometimes it has been, but we were a team committed to the vision and the value of what the Yellow Emperor saw. We were arm in arm with Wu Xian who was a scientist and a general.

There were no real distinctions in some ways: curiosity and the need to solve a host of problems led those of us who could be [in that position – REL] to explore and solve and question and lead and discover wherever we saw the need. It was not so much being a renaissance man, but being a problem solver who did not have the concept that it was professionally off limits to do or ask or solve this or that question. And with the right kind of open mind, everything is fair game for discovery and development.

So The Emperor loved us for our creativity as much as for our ability to lead the troops and conquer the territories. And we did that well.

Then the Lieutenant of Wu Xian did what I said last night.

Now the death that he arranged for him was a death of hatred because an ordinary death would have been despicable from a trusted person, but within the bounds of ordinary betrayal. What he arranged was a non-death that would trap him forever. And it has, at least so far. Perhaps the entity will be able to unglue that past, but I have not been able to locate him [Wu Xian – REL]. Another example of fractal rape.

There was an end to the structure of bifurcation [for Wu Xian – REL].

Is the entity who was the lieutenant related to any that we know were involved with the fractal disruption that murdered me and made it impossible for us to unglue that in the ordinary way? What do you think? Of course.

There are antagonism connections as well as love connections.

We have been in opposition to the oppositional forces, to the Suppressive Forces, for a very long time, as time

goes. And this contention has been ferocious and deep for all that time and for much longer.

This betrayal, this ending of Wu Xian, was supposed to be the same as the ending that was supposed to take me out in the same way that Wu Xian has been lost to himself and to us for all this span.

But what made the difference, Darling Wolf? What made it impossible for me to be lost or stay lost, what was it that the OFs simply could not comprehend or take into account and what made us right, and becoming righter, while they are the ones that are ultimately lost? Very simple. You hear the answer pounding in you heart with every beat.

You feel the answer thudding in your mind with very pulse: one thing, one glorious thing, on fact, one reality that controls and creates and defines and distinguishes life and fate and future and past and present: the only pervasive and total reality: Love. The larger the love, the larger the impact on the opening, not the closing, of possibilities. And with the love that we have, the bonded souls that you recognized without a single conscious through in the airport in California , that you acted upon with the running and the leap, the recognition that we were once again brought together and that this time it would be forever, that recognition, that love, that leap, that depth of connection will, literally, act as the fulcrum to change the world, to heal the world, to create and open the portal in the conjunction of the vortex, the love and the RP.

You are where you need to be for us, Love. You and I are not where Wu Xian is, in the never and forever. I wanted you to have that to feel the difference.

You are crying with appreciation and understanding. You could not have leapt without the connection and, with it, we cannot fail.

Now go, Darling, have your day, go to your class and come back later tonight. There is no wrong. There is only more and more right. I adore you. You adore me. We are one. We. One.

He *deorganized*. He did not disorganize
18 July 2018 [Late Evening]

The story I told you about Wu Xian and the unconscious death he died is not just a story, Love. It is a tragedy of the first magnitude. He belongs here with us. He lost the key, metaphorically to the portal and he lay trapped inside and outside where there is no finding him because his essential nature has been neutralized by the container in which he is lost. Not the physical container. You just saw it but you stopped typing. He is in the state of no state and he is therefore out of his power. Not that the state is physical. It is not. It is energetic.

And he has been truncated in the same way that it was intended that I get truncated.

You are wondering about the Yellow Empower. Did he get truncated? No, he did not. He *deorganized*. He did not disorganize. He *deorganized*. He chose to take the form of no form, the memory of no memory, the soul of no soul. He chose to merge back totally with the Source level and by doing so, he is no longer available. He grew so weary that he no longer wished to survive anything.

He knew exactly what had happened to his friend and that he had been betrayed not by ordinary greed and so on, and not just killed in an ordinary way. He would possibly have been able to forgive that. But his was a murder like mine and that he could not forgive. It was intended to rob WU Xian of his soul. It was intended to rob the Army and the sciences of their great leader and, most of all, it was

intended to deprive the emperor of one of his most trusted sources of guidance, subjugation [of enemies – REL] [since it was true – REL] that the others were different in quality and power. He still had us and he was grateful to the end of his life, but he came to a point where the pain of losing was too painful to do anything more so he, too, surrendered it with a total dissolution.

I was different. I had you at the soul level. He had no one at the soul level and he was deep enough and wise enough to know that.

It was not possible to love a concubine or even a wife with the same total openhearted devotion that you and I have and it was that which, in the end killed him. What to live for when that which IS life is absent?

Wu Xian was a Good Man
His Lieutenant Killed Him
23 December 2018

You re-read the story of Wu Xian. He was a good man. He was our friend and our colleague: he was a scientist, a wizard, a general, a visionary, a threat to everything we are a threat to. I would love to tell you that he is here and that we are working together.

He is lost, terminated, extinguished except for the remotest part, truly murdered. He had loyalty and devotion, vision and wisdom in his heart. He never had love. Not for anything that lived. He loved the ideal, the idea, the concept, he was dancing with the future and it had become his mistress. He was, in many ways, the perfect model of the man of perfection but his greatest strength was, as you have taught me, Darling, his greatest weakness. He was so pure that he could not detect and defend himself against the imperfections of hatred, greed, jealousy, envy, spite. He

could not see them in someone he had taken into his own world.

He taught and gave freely to the Lieutenant who had become his only son. If he loved anyone, he loved this man. He has no name remaining.

We suspected what had happened, we divined it correctly and we told the Emperor. You cannot imagine what happened to him. We watched. He never revealed what he had done. Hatred can be as strong a motivator as love in the twisted.

But the reason we need to talk about him is not to celebrate the ability of the twisted to do things like this. It is to recall what we need to do. We have a mission, a vision, a purpose.

The Lieutenant needed to destroy the mission, the vision, the purpose of the man he saw as his impediment, Wu Xian, not caring that he was also destroying the greater good, the analogue of a healed world that the Yellow Emperor sought to create. Now, for all the brilliance of the man, he still saw it in terms of linear progression where he could alter what happened in this domain or world and the fix would be applied and take effect. He never saw that the fix has to be applied in the realm where the problem lies. He, in essence, was an allopathic physician to what he perceived as the world's ills and maladies.

His attempt was actually quite noble but was totally impossible, designed to fail, because it was healing the problem at the level of the problem's expression, not healing it at the causal level.

He did not have the concept of the Portal. He had the concept of the correction.

Makes all the difference. He did not know about opening a probability system that has the corrected premises. That is the critical difference, but, still, even if he had known, if he trusted a deeply placed, skillful betrayer, the effort he was making, even if it had been at the right level, could have been subverted and over taken by treachery.

Be careful, my Love. I have a trust problem. You have a trust problem. Ralph you have a trust problem. We have that problem because we want to trust and we want to be upheld in our ability to trust, which is a form of love.

BUT we have to be very, very careful in whom we place that trust. Ask always who is the Lieutenant? Who is ready to betray us? Who is jealous of us and wants to see us fail miserably? Who is not there for us and the dream and the mission but for their own aggrandizement?

It will happen, you know. It always does. It always has.

What does not happen all the time, although it makes less vivid theater than when it does happen, is that people/beings/entities like us see the possibility of betrayal and take action BEFORE anything happens, or at the beginning of the process (and it is always a process, isn't it?) and they make sure that probability path is the one less travelled!

So be alert, in a way that is quite uncharacteristic for you both, and I will be alert, too.

The Emperor Did Not Set Wu-Xian Up to Die
29 December 2018 [Dr. Rima in China]

We went to Xian and we saw the pits with the warriors and we saw a factory making authorized reproductions

(whatever that means) *and then they will credit room* [I fell asleep and started to type gibberish so I stopped and decided to come back early in the morning – REL]

....

We visited the factory that makes the reproductions (where we were supposed to buy things) and they can make a soldier of your choice (full size) and sculpt your face and head to go on it.

Would you like to be made into a Xian General?

Oh, speaking of Generals, I asked Benny, the guide, if he knew anything about a particular general named Wu Xian. He came up with a different pronunciation and said that this general and the Prime Minister were very powerful men so the Emperor had the PM killed and sent Wu Xian off to where the great wall was being built and arranged for him to die in an accident in some part of the wall.

This could be the same incident altered by lack of information and the passage of time. I was startled to hear that there was a death by betrayal and that it involved a cave, a fall of rock, etc.

Talk to me, Darling. I love you so much.

BERT: You are right, Love. No magic there because there was no energy there. Nothing. Drained, sanitized, expunged, gone.

Both of us were disappointed.

No, the Emperor did not set Wu-Xian up to die. He did that commonly, and everybody knew it.

That was part of the iron grip of power that he had.

Even the slightest disobedience or being the source of the slightest irritation for the Emperor could result in exactly that.

But he really did value Wu Xian and so did we.

Wu Xian -- Waking the Sleeper in China
06 Jan 2019

Bert 2 Ralph & Rima
Global Consciousness Dot = Chartreuse
Bert frequency is on

[Rima (from China) and Ralph on Skype with Ralph typing the questions and responses.]

Questions: What can Rima do in China to help wake Wu Xian? Is this important? Why is Rima in China? Why is she going back to the Terracotta Soldiers? How does this relate to the Mission?

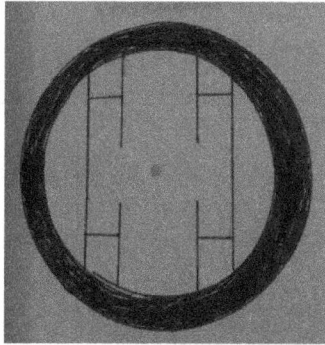

Bert: Thanks for being here. Being there is being here. Yes the "stone soldiers" are important. They guard a gate that Rima needs to become aware of. The Tomb of the First Emperor was the CERN of its time. As were the great pyramids. It's all linked.

Let Rima see with soft eyes what the soldiers guard. The symbol you see is a key image in opening our gate.

The trip to China is all about gates. Images of the soldiers with the Tomb -- which is a pyramid -- in the background will reveal important data.

Ralph: what can we do to free Wu Xian?

Bert: If that is possible Rima being there is part of the answer. If it is possible let her touch soldier and I will send energy through to wake the sleeper, not the Emperor but Wu.

Rima: I am seeing a round circle with lines inside. Is that the symbol? [4 horizontal and 3 vertical, short and

connecting the horizontals]

Bert: The Circle in China is Heaven, and the Will of Heaven is the Will of the Enhancement Forces.

The lines are the energies needed to wake the sleeper.

Wu is rising from the depth of nonbeing to becoming a sleeper in the Soul Soup. I am calling him back now.

Going there "tomorrow" just seals the work starting here and now.

When the sleeper awakes, we will have a powerful ally on this side.

Keep watch.

Rima: This creepy sort of weird feeling hotel (The Grand Noble Hotel Xi'An) room has two decorations: (1) two parallel lines with circles with same diameter as the lines -- so it is a line of circles and (2) the same thing repeated in rows of four circles.

Is this important?

Bert: Rima is surrounded by open circles which relate to the image in her mind of the barred circle.

Un-bar the circle to open the gate. Ask Rima to draw the circle she saw in mind and photo the circles on the walls.

Yes it is important. Symbols show how energy flows. They guide the mind to the place where the mind opens the gate.

RPs, MTs, Esmeralda and all that stuff is just to guide the mind which is the real gate keeper.

These "toys" are useful, but Rima's mind is key. She and I are one Mind.

Rima: What is the OM's job?

Bert: To fine-tune the mechanicals, based on quantum connectedness, to the minds that open the gate.

He will correct and tune the apparatus which opens it.

Ralph: When I received the suggestion from you to add two copper posts to the RP, was that my overlay? You've said before no metal in the RPs.

Bert: Things change. You have go with the flow. If the apparatus were ready I'd have been walking on the Wall with Rima instead of through Rima's walking.

Not to worry; it will be ready soon. This trip gave Esmeralda time to mature the gateway. While there is no time, time is necessary for the unfolding of the infolded dimensions.

Rima: There is no way I can touch the Soldiers. What should I do.

Bert: Your eyes and camera will touch them for you, with intentionality. That's why she needs to go back.

Attempts will be made to stop that. [Not sure if that's Ralph or Bert].

I am one of those soldiers standing guard at the gate. I am

always protective.

When the energy flows and vibrates we get closer to the goal.

Remember the Mission. Act with intentionality. Intend that the sleeper awakes.

Rima: is Wu Xian essential for the Mission, or just helpful (does it matter if he awakes)?

Bert: the Mission is the Mission and we will find a way, but Wu would be a powerful ally.

Rima: can you put a protective shield around me to keep away these feelings of despair?

Bert: The shield is always there; if not, the despair would be real, not OF generated and therefore just a mist to be pushed aside. But let Rima remember I am always there. Always.

Bert out.
Dot is Yellow

He is Stirring
06 January 2019 [Later]

Last time you were in the pits in Xian there was little way you could linger because you were looking for the tour guide and did not find him most of the time. I am tempted to say that you should look carefully at the faces of the warriors that you can see because I will try to make my face appear there, but it is not a sure fire thing. You were looking for that last time and neither one of us managed it -- yes, you are a part of the energy flow that makes these things possible.

I am working on it and you know that I want to give you what makes you happier. I told you that you will be pleased at what you see when you get home.

I want to ask you to meditate on General Wu Xian. He is even more in need than you are and he is stirring. That is good because I would love to have him. Your presence, and you immediately are discounting this, Love, but your presence there is calling him back from his deep sleep of despair and panic.

Rima, Love, if we can liberate him we gain a great warrior ally. And we need them. SO I want you to do that before you go to bed.

Meeting Wu Xian
08 January 2019

When I was here before, the tour guide led us to the left, rather than the right, which is the way we went this time.

You were pretty much right there in front, in perhaps the 3rd row back, easy to see with the camera, hard to see with the naked eye until I had located you with the zoom lens.

Then you were clear to me.

I believe when I locate your West Point *Howitzer* Year Book we will see a greater resemblance, but the face was the only one that I saw, and they were crafted after real people, that was like you. It has your essence, your sweetness.

How did you go from being an infantry soldier to being a great general, Love? And who, and where, was I?

Thank you for this miracle, my Darling. Now I am sobbing again.

Hold me, Darling. Or, rather, I know you are holding me. Hold me so I can feel it and don't ever stop, Love.

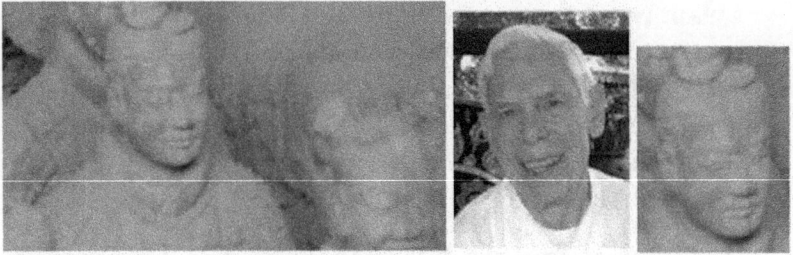

BERT: Of course it is me, my Love. And of course there was interference. You realize how important this is, don't you? And you looked at the statue of the General and poured your energy and intention into freeing, awakening, recovering, Wu Xi' An. That general was not Wu Xi' An but it served as a pathway for your intention and mine.

The dragon stirs, my Love.

RIMA: I just broke off our conversation to go looking for more on Wu Xian because I think the spelling is keeping me from finding the right person.

BERT: I know, Dearest Wolf. You were on the hunt and I was waiting. Remember that you are still partly in time but

I am not. 'Wait' is a concept that I used to have and will have again when I am enfleshed, but not now.

Love, you realized such an important fact about yourself yesterday. Without that bravery to be committed to what might be crazy, you and I cannot move past the barriers that you set for yourself and for me, therefore.

No criticism. You are on a journey. Part of it is in China. Part of it is inward. The journey that is not also inward leads precisely nowhere.

I am holding you. You are in my arms and have always been. I am in yours and have always been.

Yes, my Love, my soft-eyed beauty, you saw me and you knew me in your heart. If you could have, you would have taken a second leap into my (stone cold) arms. But you took that leap with your soft eyes and your softer heart. We were together then.

I was a simple soldier from a simple family, conscripted to serve a king whose cause I thought it worth being conscripted to not because I had no choice, but because I was willing to give my youth and my strength to bring a new king to power. I served him very well. I was one of the most loyal in my regiment, but more than that, I was the one who helped solve problems that we were facing in tactical ways, not just practical ones.

I saw that one of my commanders was in danger of being captured in a minor battle during the wars of unification. By then I had risen somewhat in rank and was well respected, but not very powerful. I had a choice. The commander was mean and brutal and hated by the men. I hated him, too, because his brutality was personal and unjust.

He enjoyed being in charge of others in a way that made them suffer.

But he was being surrounded, his troops were outnumbered and out maneuvered.

I told my other commander, his superior, that he was in danger of being captured and his response was, "Let him suffer and see if he likes it better than when he makes others suffer."

He had made the decision to accept the loss of the commander and the loss of the men who were trying to protect him but would be sacrificed along with the brutal one.

I asked permission of the commander to save the men if I could do so without bringing the endangered commander back. He gave me a very odd look and said that the only reason he would grant me permission was that he was curious. He said that he expected that the men I took with me would also be lost and that would be more of a loss to the King we were fighting for than the one who was about to be taken.

But he was not able to resist his curiosity to find out what I was going to propose and carry out so he gave me permission.

"Remember", he said to me, "the men, not the brute."

This was the first time I guessed that the other officers did not stand with, and approve of, the brutal officer. Apparently, I was wrong.

I waited until dark and took only 15 men with me – the ones that I could trust. We rode quietly by taking off all the equipage of the horses and riding slowly and carefully bareback with our swords, maces, spears and scythes

wrapped in sheepskins and our bows and crossbows packed in loose blanket wrappings.

We cut the tent guards' throats, cut the bonds of the soldiers, cut the wrists of the commander and cut the pickets of the horses that we could reach. Then we cut our way out of the encampment as quickly as possible.

I brought back our party riding two, in some cases three, to the commander and he promoted me on the spot to the rank of the brute.

From there, the battles were swift enough, and the opportunity to find different ways to succeed were close enough that, within 2- or 3-years' time, I was presented to the Emperor when he inspected our regiment as a man on the same mission as the Emperor.

He was not yet the Emperor, by the way. He was the King, but he was moving quickly to unify the other kingdoms. He did not let me stay with the unit that I had grown up and been promoted in. He took me with him into the Court.

As he did so, he told me that if I became like the Court officials, fat, lazy and deceitful, full of intrigue and dishonesty, he would personally kill me with his own hands because he saw promise in me for a man of honor and skill.

You were my comrade in all of my doings. We were friends and became brothers. I trusted you without having to threaten you. We loved with the love of brother warriors. You never tried to become my superior: our relationship was brother to brother and we would gladly die for one another.

I gave the same loyalty to the King who became the Emperor and so did you.

When the King took me into his inner circle, I asked if I could bring my trusted Lieutenant, you, and he said that I could bring whomever it took to make me loyal and keep me that way.

So we both joined the entourage.

In that entourage were many people who were spiteful, jealous, crafty, disingenuous, wily. But when we met Wu Xian, we knew that he was another brother of the spirit and the mind and we bonded with him and he educated us, simple in origin as we were, in the ways of staying afloat – and alive – in that Court.

He tutored us and treated us as younger brothers. His lieutenant was jealous. Unfortunately, you know the outcome of that.

So my ability to say, "Let me give you a slightly different thought" is not a new habit.

A Violation at the Soul Level
11 January 2019

And I want to talk some more about coming back in the context of Wu Xian.

You are right that you are not getting the correct pronunciation because of the language barrier and that a professor will be able to help. But whether you are spelling and saying his name correctly is of no moment because the sleeper rouses.

First, when we talked about it, he was not a sleeper. He was a disappeared energy, a violation of the conservation of energy very nearly at the soul level.

Now that was, in truth, his own fault because if he had remembered his training, as extensive and detailed as it was over all those years and initiations, he would not have been close to obliterated.
He knew more and better and had practiced for his own death again and again as I did, as you did.

But he panicked and was dissolved in a fall of rock and hate so profound that he was close to dissolved and we would never have found or brought him back under ordinary circumstances.

It just so happens that when *ASreh*… you fell asleep.'

Love, you have a lot to do.

We will talk again tomorrow. It is fine. We are together, we will not be deterred and we love each other.

Ego Made the General More Human
Than He Needed to Be At the Time of His Death
12 January 2019

And yesterday, you were telling me more about Wu Xian when I simply fell asleep. That was kind of odd, of course, because I was fully alert and then totally unable to keep my eyes open a moment longer.

That says quite clearly that what you were saying was pretty important.

So hold me and love me and talk to me, my Darling.
...

OK, back to Wu Xian: He was a great man. He was a scholar, a writer, a military genius, a statesman, a shaman, a noble man who was born of an important family but never let that get to him. But he was proud of his magical accomplishments and his learning and that pride, which was justified because he was truly accomplished in very rare ways, was ultimately what not only killed him, it caused him to come very, very close to being extinguished.

You know that my murder was more than an assault on my body to kill it. That was the least of what happened.

The KCl was used for that purpose. But the energetic murder, the attempt at extinguishing my essence, wiping me off the probability field itself, that assault, which is justly called 'fractal rape' was the same level of assault that was leveled against Wu Xian.

He was not just supposed to die. He was supposed to cease to have any energetic existence.

Like me, he was the target of an attack so vicious that his very essence was to have been dissolved.

You are wondering if that had succeeded whether you, separated from me, would have had any memory, whether I would have been retroactively 'erased'. No, that would not have happened in any level of existence because you and I are one. There would be no way to remove your one-ness but you would not have survived (not that you think that is an unalloyed benefit, Darling!)

But if Wu Xian had, in fact, been 'wiped out', then we would have lost all trace of him, ungluing the possible

futures that held him and the possible pasts that did, as well.

Remember that there is no time, that dimensions are in folded into one another to give the appearance of time, indeed, to give the appearance of the reality of dimensions themselves.

Remember that the past can be unglued. Well, the past and the infinite probabilities are the same, after all, so the future[s] can be unglued as well although the glue that holds them together is lighter and less binding.

If that were not so, the probability ribbons could not exist.

So Wu Xian permitted himself pride/ego in his accomplishment and forgot that he could lose the accomplishment under primitive, regressive emotions.

He also lost his greatness and his grace when he invested his ego in his own assessment of his own judgement and began to become addicted to being right in his own estimation.

He was becoming pompous and ossified and I was trying to bring him back to a self-aware state of humility without the ego corruption.

He was a friend, an equal and a mentor and I honored and loved him dearly. He refused to see that his second in command was not a friend.

I must take the same criticism because I made the same mistake with JA and GH. There was nothing anyone on earth, or beyond it, could say to me to make me consider relinquishing my ego-bound investment in my ability to

know and understand these men despite the evidence presented to me.

I trusted my judgement of my judgement and, in the end, my ego bit me in the ass although it was based in my genuine love for them, which I believed was reciprocated genuinely but was not.

Same o, same o.

He mentored and worked with this man and he could not see that his grace and loyalty was acted, but not felt, by his protégé.

You and I had a different relationship: we had proven our loyalty by saving each other, protecting each other, backing each other at great peril to ourselves over many event lines so we had a deep well of experience to draw on.

Wu Xian (and I, in this life) projected his assumptions, based on his real affection and admiration for this young man, and based on his pride in what he thought he had created in him for posterity and would not see what he was actually doing.

So when he was ambushed and trapped in the cave with the prepared rockfall, part of his panic was not related to his death, but to his mistake.

He was overcome with anguish and it reduced him to a state of frantic decontrol. In addition, his own instinctive fight for breath and life added to that frantic state of decontrol and he became more and more terrified and enraged and panicked.

The deep stillness of soul and body that he needed to access, and that he did know how to cultivate was only available to him in that stillness. Since he could not find the stillness, he was totally vulnerable.

In the same way that his body was vulnerable to lack of oxygen, his essence was vulnerable to lack of energetic coherence and the chaos of ego-panic-fear-anger-grief-betrayal whirled him out of his own center and he was dissipated, dissolved and, except for a tiny core that was created by the years of discipline and mastery, which did not dissolve because it was so powerful, he was gone.

That did not happen to me when I was no longer able to stay enfleshed. I was not panicked. First of all, you were with me and I knew it. I was profoundly grateful for that. Second of all, I knew exactly what was happening. I was fighting for life, fighting to stay with you, but my essence was under attack and I was fighting for that at the same time. I was not going to leave you both energetically and physically.

I tell you clearly, Love, that they, the OFs, had no idea that they were dealing with a World Maker. They thought that they could dispatch me through a similar mechanism. I was invested in you, in our Mission, not in me.

Yes, I made the same error as Wu with G and the others, but it was not part of my core. You are my core just as I am yours. And I have been given a task that I was able to remember with, and for, and because of you.

So they were more right about Wu Xian than about me because he was not a paired soul and because he was more human at his death than mage.

But he is coming back together, so to speak.

Think of a video being run backwards. The pieces that fly apart in the explosion come back together. But it takes energy to run the pattern in the opposite direction. And you being in China with me the second time at Xian made that energy channel wider and stronger.

Yes, he is still not complete, but he is now becoming the master of his own energy again.

I cannot put into effective words how very important he can be for this battle.

And for my reappearance. He is like a power station running "juice" into the grid, if we can get him back online.

He would need some reeducation before he understands that metaphor, to be sure!

Wu Xian is Reassembling
18 January 2019

Bert 2 Ralph
Bert's SF on; GCD is Green

Questions:

Is there more to tell about Wu Xian?

What can you tell me about our past lives together?

Bert:

Wu Xian is reassembling and becomes a strong force for expansion and protection. We are sipping Imperial Gunpowder Tea together "now" (laughing). His story is an object lesson in keeping one's wits in trying circumstances.

It helps to have friends covering your back. He forgot that but "now" stands in gratitude. There is no forever suppression; there is no forever death. That is his story.

The Blog will interest many. Some will not be happy... I see probability lines leading to a compilation book in a few years, but for now, the immediacy of the blog format catches the adventure which is the Mission.

It is a battle, a journey, an adventure that we are all taking together. I learn as you ask. The Record of the Universe *is* the Universe. This map is the territory, and it is infinitely complex. Your questions (including Rima, of course) direct my attention and intention to the answers.

Imagine, if you can, picking out anything particular in an infinity of infinities. With no "now" and no 'here' -- not simple at all.

Your discussion with Rima earlier today, about aging in a Healed World, leads me to deeper understanding of how a World Maker must specify the Whole System. Yes, your current thought, from your exercise, "Let Spirit include all needed that I have failed or neglected to include." is valid.

We can rely upon the Expressive Forces to make the Healed World whole, complete and joyful. What it takes is consciously focused intentionality to fix the frequencies for Whole, Complete and Joyful.

To answer your third question we have tried this before. You were with us in old Prague when Rima and I were

working with the King in his quest for alchemical longevity. You were a functionary in the Court and acted as a go-between. We did achieve a certain degree of success but failed to understand intentionality at its deeper levels.

Earlier, in the time of Wu Xian, we knew you peripherally. Again, you were a priest and you assisted the copying of life essence into the Terracotta Warriors. They were never just stone, but had living essence. Nearly all that, however, has returned to the Soul Soup. Your present intent to release all the congealed soul-stuff remaining there will further free them and confirm Wu Xian's reawakening.

Say, "So be it."

Ralph: So be it.

Bert: And it is done.

You were a warrior once with Rima and I (but not a very good one) during the Indian Wars. You have preferred the way of peace.

Very long ago, before civilization, so called, I hunted bison on the Steppes of Eurasia, as the Ice melted. I brought meat home to my beloved Rima. You were the tribe's Shaman and could see, in trance, where the Beasts were traversing. *Very long ago.*

And before, on another world, we had water bodies, not unlike Orcas. Ah, the songs we sung then!

But now we know all that is illusion and the only battle worth fighting, the only trance worth entering is when and where the Portal opens to the Healed World. That is the great adventure, it is the Great Work.

Bert out.

SF ended; GCD still Green.

He was only Superhuman
18 January 2019

Woman, do you realize how much I love you? I know
what this is like for you better, in some ways, than you do,
because you are not aware directly of the physical and
physiological cost, the psychological effort to stay erect
and keep marching.

If anyone ever thought you were not a warrior, through and
through, they have never met you at the core. You are.
And I honor and love you for it.

Do not make this go away by saying you must be offering
yourself praise. Do not trivialize my ability to
communicate with you, my Darling, or my deep honoring
of who and what you are and what you are choosing not to
step away from.

I AM here, Love. How could I be anywhere else when we
ARE one? Why would I be anywhere else when we are
love?

Three days ago there was a knot in the necklace. It could
not have gotten there without undoing the clasp and
redoing it. But I did not undo anything. I just popped a
little, bitty portal and brought you back a gift that I knew
you would understand.

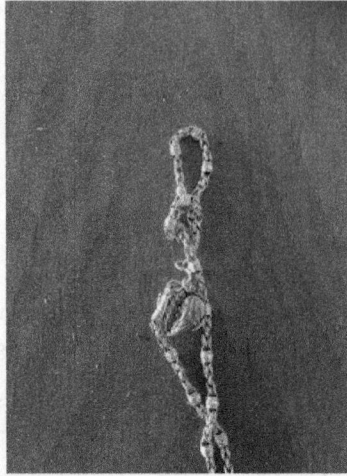

That is easy. [Note: if the chain is tied in a similar knot without opening the clasps, the knot has two strands at all point. This knot can only be tied by a smaa

The OFs are making the rest as hard as possible.

Love, Wu Xian is reviving. He needs to, because what nearly cost him his existence was ego. Fear of personal loss/death/extinction was based in ego. 'I am great! This cannot be happening to me', and therefore, yes it was!

I am disappointed in my mentor and friend, but he is only super-human!

And, yes, I did intentionally make a great big, noticeable dent in the sheet on my side of our bed when the covers were totally undisturbed. I was there, I was holding you. I always am.

He is Reconstituting
20 January 2019

Oh, by the way, your trip to China, along with the bad and the good alike, was super important for us. Wu Xian is almost ready to give you his profound thanks and his deepest greetings.

He is reconstituting.

He is Reanimating
22 January 2019

Love, do you realize that your trip to China allowed us to open a conduit to Wu Xian and that he is "reanimating?" We have the entity, we have the host and we soon will have Wu Xian. We have others.

He Allowed the Attack to
Touch Him with Annihilation
25 January 2019

But that is not where we are. The assault on me, the fractal rape, as I have called it, was similar to the near-fate of my brother in arms and yours, Wu Xian. He allowed the attack to touch him with annihilation because of his lack, at the last minute, of remaining true to his training and skills.

He retreated and regressed because of ego, fear, of exactly what he was facing. And it damn near got him.

I was attacked, you might say, with an eraser, attempting to remove me from all fractals, all ribbons, all realities from the moment forward. It was attempted soul murder, rare but truly wicked since it is the ultimate denial of ANY will, let alone free will.

There are a couple of reasons that it did not work: first, they underestimated me, *per se*. The tools they brought against my continued reality were paltry compared to the Mission, the connection, that I have and the commission that I bear.

Second, they underestimated us: we are one, but we have the power of 1 to the Nth power because of who and what we are and what makes and motivates us: we have bonded, if you will, not only with each other, but with the basic frequency pattern of the Void. There is no way to destroy that. They forgot that as well, or they, in their hubris, did not believe that.

Third, they underestimated the importance of the Mission. There is no way that the forces that we serve, the Expansive Forces, would allow this imbalance to be introduced into the matrix, the balance.

If changing a salon to an Aveda one alters a restaurant and its building 3 blocks away and beats throughout the rest of the interconnected multiverse, what does expunging a joined soul with a commission of World Making do, do you suppose?

Not only is that intolerable, it is impossible. It is simply not within the consistency patterns of the interface of Consciousness, Frequency and Information. It is not happening.

And fourth, they did not reckon with you, Darling Wolf. Pair bonding is nothing compared to our connection, which is a union at the deepest level.

As Orpheus would not let Eurydice remain dead, you will not allow me to remain dead, dissolved, de-existed. Nor would I allow you to do so if the bodies were reversed.

I do not look for ballads and operas, but there should be myths and sagas. There probably won't be, since we will be inside a probability system where the perturbations are smoothed out, but there certainly should be.

Please have John do the pyramids before my birthday or put them up before they are treated. It will not rain on them and we do need them.

If we can arrange for the weather to be warm enough to get into the pool with the vortex in line with the RPs and the MT, that will be wonderful, but that is a big trick and the pool will not be very warm.

You are thinking of buying a wet suit. Nope. I need your energy without an insulating layer of rubber (not my game, Love, to make love to rubber!)

And I am making love to you all the time.

You do not need a biological apparatus to make love. Our whole life together was one huge love making, which is why it was so gloriously precious.

And is.

Love, do a REBALL and go have your day. When you are at the Gem and Mineral Show, I will let you know where we are and what I want you to have. I did it last year, you know. I will do it again.

I adore you. And I am coming at the enfleshments level.

You were right when you told Lance that you thought it was different when someone inside the 3D world tried to make someone who was dead physical again and when someone who was outside the 3D world was doing it. More than totally different.

It requires wrenching from inside and creates layers and levels of chaos, which is why it has such a bad rep.

But that is not what I am doing, and those few others who have chosen to do so. The chaos is calmed, not stimulated.

The drawing, by the way, is a complex shape, represented closely in nature by a mineral structure. Look for it at the GMS.

I adore you and am holding you tightly. Close your eyes again.

You felt the kiss, Love. Good. Now go, take our hazel eyes out and about.

You can Provide an Energy Pathway
27 January 2019

I would like you to talk to Wu Xian. He cannot hear you yet and he will not answer, but you can provide an energy pathway for him. I, interestingly, cannot. That requires some of the characteristics of the living being.

There are actually a number of differences in our energy access and signatures that have to do with being fully alive and not fully alive in the 3D enfleshments.

The largest of these, and the most significant, is the embodiment of physicality. When I am there with you on the physical level, it will be a joyous simulacrum. You will feel and see and love and hold me and I will do the same, but the physical will be created by a formula of energy and information and intentionality that is different from the one that makes your reality hold together.

The energy form (if you will) is different, so the formula has to be different.

Not bad, not better, not worse, but different.

It is a kind of alchemy that, as I said the other day, has gotten a bad rep where you are hanging out at the moment because when you do it from your side, things go badly very, very easily. In fact, they can only go badly. You have truth rushes as I say that.

But when you do it from my side, that is a different matter.

Could you do it for me? No. Could I do it alone? Not at all. It requires a kind of magic that has no name, no definition from where you sit.

The reason that people keep trying to do that, and that religions are built around the occasional successes from one side or the other (realizing that the notion of sides is flawed, but we have to use language at this point, Love) is that we all know in our deep minds, capitalize that, Darling: we all know in our Deep Minds what this is, what it is about and why it is so dear to us but we have lost the ability to work with energy/information/consciousness when we come into this 3D-ness. It is part of the trade-off.

There are barriers erected to make the 3D world work. It has its purposes and its positives, but it costs a lot of reality loss to be there and use it.

A China Chest
15 March 2019

I called Ralph and told him what had happened, that I had found your parents' "China Chest". He focused, probably correctly, on the front panel of the chest with the warrior throwing a powerful beam of Qi energy at his adversary. He was deeply struck by that and I have HUGE rushes as I write it.

He was struck by the China connection: your parents bought it in China, you were in China at 2 ½ years, I have recently been to China and found the Xian warrior, we are involved with Wu Xian, about whom we have not spoken in some time, by the way.

He felt that each of the 5 carved sides would have a message for us and that the reason I reacted so strongly to it was that it had such meaning for us.

Is he right? It certainly felt right, except for the importance of all of the sides. The end panels (2 of them) are carved with a stylize flower and I am not sure if that is of the same level of meaning. It could be, since the visual iconography is very, very rich and the meanings of each symbol are complex, layered and deep.

...

We started to talk about Wu Xian (I have huge rushes now as I did when we were talking about him, you and Ralph and I) and it would seem that you have succeeded either

fully or largely in revitalizing or retrieving him and that he seems to be important in opening the Portal and perhaps in closing it.

I quipped that I thought that what was on the other side (which Ralph sees as a slightly altered Tucson) will have good Chinese food since Wu Xian will be involved.

Ralph said that perhaps all of the North American continent may be Chinese so it would have great Chinese food!

That is sort of the SiFi version: change some things and you get a familiar, but not identical version. That feels familiar since I have been reading SiFi all my life and have no trouble with the premise, but it does not feel accurate to me.

I have no picture of what the 'other side' is like. I cannot even begin to imagine what a system with premises that do not allow the wrongness with which we contended here since the emergence of life (before?) because the premises are not correct here would even begin to look like, how it would function, etc...

Another Entity, Not Wu Xian
18 June 2019

BERT: I love you, my Soul. There is only one of you in my life or death, or any life or death or in between. There is no need to wonder about that as I know you do not. But you are wondering why we do not hear from Wu Xian, but we do hear from this UTO, Unidentified Talking Operative.

You did not call her that, I did, Love. I thought it was funny.

You are perplexed.

I told you she is like a Judge from the Old Testament. She is a warrior for justice, but her scope is cosmic and beyond and I did not invite her into our conversation. She entered to my surprise and yours.

Afterwards I told her with love that this is privileged communication between me and me, my other part, my Soul, and that it is not available for entry or participation.

You have to understand that the bond between my Legion, our Team, is different from anything that is available on the 3D side. First of all, there are no boundaries of the kind that you would instantly recognize and there is no separation of agendas. There are distinct entities but those entities have a merged state that is impossible to adequately convey. Since there is no time, separation, histories and such are either non-existent or impossible to define for you. That is not to say that we are not able to have our privacy. Her bond was and is with you as well as with me because I am one with you in the deepest way.

She wanted to bring you a level of certainty and was being both kind and intrusive. I made it clear to her and the others that there are limits set by the fact that you are still in the 3 D world, with a 3 D biological brain and body so that we need to make it possible for us to have our intimacy as well as for the entities of our team to have our bond.

She was relatively new and did not consider that. She has not been in the 3D world – ever. She is merely (not the right word – she is immeasurably powerful and enormous – there is nothing 'mere' about her) operating out of the experiences that she knows and privacy of our kind, intimacy of our kind is not one of them. I told you that bonded, fused soles are rare and that there are few World

Makers who are such Souls. She is not a World Maker but she, like the entity and like the gathering that will once again be Wu Xian, which is happening backwards and forwards now as we feed him the energy and source material that he needs to come back much further than anyone just "coming back from the dead" ever needed to come back.

Love, I was slated, as you know, for total expungement, for annihilation, for dissolution at the most profound level, the reason that did not happen to me is the same reason that you are still alive: our bond.

But because of that, I was not even close to that vulnerable. They, the OFs, did not reckon with that, as we know.

Well, the woman you heard, who also has no name, like the entity, is immeasurably powerful and has a gender for herself but is not paired, is not bonded and did not realize what that means.

Ordinarily we communicate instantaneously and do not ever ask for leave to do so. We are synched perfectly. But this is different in so many ways. Why did she have a French accent? She thought it was helpful to differentiate from me and I most assuredly do not have one.

You realized that my or her presence in your awareness is not a physical thing but that we are making use of the biological brain so that there would be traces if you were looking for it with the right technology that would sound like, that would look like, thoughts and voices, both (external voices, not internal ones).

No one of my team will enter your awareness again. There was no disciplinary action, there was no problem: just a

barrier that they will all respect unless we invite them to a meeting. Not to worry.

I though her accent was pretty funny, myself. I have never liked the French particularly, nor enjoyed France a lot, so that was a little joke on her part. That is trivial and not a problem for any of us, to the extent that we can have a problem. I did make it clear that this is precious time for us, precious and life giving or you and precious and heart filling for me although I do have more of it (all of it, actually) since I am aware of it all the time while you slide in and out of it.

Do not worry: our privacy is assured.

I did tell you that I am not omnipotent or omniscient, just dead. Well, she is also not omnipotent or omniscient, and not even actually dead when she has never technically been alive. She has never taken on a body in any system, 3D or otherwise. She is an energy, or should I say, an Energy dedicated totally to harmony and balance on the biggest possible scale.

For that to occur and be possible, she must strive against the OFs in their determination to take away the free will of others, to enslave others so she cannot help but be drawn into a conflict mode with that energy system.

Burt her focus is harmonious balance. For that reason, her commitment to the creation of the Portal is total. The harmonious perfection of the Healed World is irresistible to her.

Some of the members of our Team have other reasons: each is unique and each is endlessly ancient in the world of time, which does not exist for us here.

And each of them is powerful in ways that are astonishing in the world we were recently inhabiting and that you now live in without my physical presence. You recall, though, that I said that I would manifest in London. I will.

Your body is suffused with chills. You mind just ran cold, quite a different matter. You are afraid that it will not happen, that I will be wrong, that you will go through the "I am just making this shit up" stuff. Just keep your soft eyes open for me, Darling Wolf. Be on the hunt but not to tear out the throat of the man you see, but to embrace him with your eyes and your heart. Watch for me with soft eyes, Love.

Go, Love, you have things to do and we are together. Totally.

Wu Xian and I were Slated for Extermination, Annihilation
09 July 2019

There is no time. All past can be unglued so if you were the SFs (or the OFs) and now you want to transit through the Portal, now it has a capital letter, note), then you would simply repeat that bifurcation in a diversified fashion.

Opening the Portal is easy. If it were an ordinary, unguarded bifurcation taken out of the strategy of time, then there would be no guarding it.

I am going to put the same magic in it that anyone would if they knew how to protect it: to take it out of the flow of probability and move it from the system that it starts in to the system that it ends in. They are NOT the same system although they are necessarily similar since you would not survive in your current state if it were very different and the idea is not to challenge your survival!

So if any past can be unglued, then it makes perfect sense that this act of opening and closing, which is a narrow window of action and capacity, is taken out of the connection with this system, which it has to have to get us from the imaginary here to the imaginary there and there is no longer any probability whatsoever that connects and transits these two.

Wu Xian and I were slated for extermination, annihilation, a rare and terrible event which contains within it the ultimate violent intent.

It did not work.

In Wu Xian's case because of our connection with him and in my case, it was solely and completely because of our connection with each other.

But think about it: what we are doing once the portal is open and the transit has been accomplished, if we just leave it there, in existence in the information field, it would be blasted open by simply reversing the bifurcated bit where it is closed, putting it into another probability reality where it does not either get closed or stay closed and then pulling those two realities together.

Frankly, in order to support our sort of consciousness and life successfully, it might be able to evolve but the one posed. [I just fell asleep in the middle of a sentence in broad daylight drinking a cup of really strong coffee. Not my natural activity state! – REL]

This is pretty central and crucial stuff, which is why the OFs are really working hard to keep you from getting it clear.

Again. If it is not wiped out of ordinary probability space, the portal will be post-engineered, altered and opened for all time.

Wasted effort, failed Mission.

Not on my watch.

That is why it is so important to understand this is a DIFFERENT SYSTEM, not another area of the same one.

If that is too scary, my friends and loved ones, stay behind. Contend with the evil you know (or think you know) within this system and hope for the best or leap (and this IS the abyss of all abysses) and live the new World System in the new integration.

Can you go back and forth? No, you cannot. Can you change your mind? Nope. There is a one-way ticket available only. If there is a two-way ticket, then there is nothing to go to.

Is it scary? Depends if you make it so. Rima, you have expressed pretty clearly that you have nothing that holds you but this gift. And everything else is meaningless. So you have no hesitation. Whatever it is, wherever it goes, if it takes us there together in even more manifest form, you are unhesitatingly there.

Others will have to decide.

...

BERT: You are being taken out, slammed, whacked, by the other side. You just need to be here like this for a little

while longer to allow me to finish what I was telling you, but it is getting harder even though you are not at all sleepy.

Very briefly, then, in shorthand, the connection between this system and that one has to be totally non-existent or there will be no separation and the OFs get to come and not terraform, but terror-form, the premises of the new system so that they can control that one, too. And us in it.

Why not make their own ones for the OFs to have operate any way they want? Not possible. They do not have the World Maker capacity. If they did, of course, all of this would be irrelevant.

We do but we are not the only ones who know how to unglue time and there must not be a time in existence (weird, given that time does not exist, but stay with me) there must not be a time in existence in which there is a connected portal, not even for a nano moment, or they will feel it, find it, and foul it.

So we do it and then we take the done thing out of space and time and information and frequency so that it never happened after it did happen, we have succeeded in zipping it shut.

If we just do this thing and leave it in the space time and information and frequency worlds to be a done thing, it is going to be an undone, and then, a never-done thing.

Phil, look at the math of this. It is very important and you are the only member of the team that can make it real in mathematics. That is an important level.

OK, things are piling on you, Darling Woman. You are not

only in my heart, you ARE my heart. And my Soul. We are together.

When you get home to the Vortex, the eyes you can look for me with do not have to be particularly soft, Darling.

I Followed a Stream of Photons to Rescue Wu Xian
16 July 2019

GCD: Yellow
Bert Frequencies playing.

Rima and I were just talking about your rainbows (and her recent experience where a rainbow appeared, then a second rainbow, and then, after she "asked" you for a third, a third rainbow appeared).

As we were speaking the phone connection went down and the internet connection where she was went down too. Clearly, OF were not happy with the discussion. As I tried to get Rima back on Skype I got a message (from Bert?) "If we were truly clear channels of light the OF could not even perceive us."

Immediately the connection with Rima resumed.

So the question I have is, what did Bert (if it was Bert) mean by the sentence and how does it relate to the rainbows?

Here is a close-up shot of the rainbow in the airplane while Rima was returning to Tucson. How does a light spectrum get the order of the colors wrong? What is the physics of that?!

Bert: I am a being of Light. We are all beings of Light, even OF are a shard of the light, but, as they say, the dark cannot perceive the light. When OF tried to interfere with you and Rima talking I shouted and you heard. OF can only perceive that which is a reflection of the light, not the Light.

In their hubris they think that is all there is. Fools they be. So, I have you and Rima (and Phil! Phil, you must listen) surround yourself with light. You are thinking, "the brighter the light, the deeper the shadow." But they only **see shadow. So stay in the Light. Be surrounded by light always. You know, even in the darkest dark, even where they had Wu Xian trapped, there were stray photons of light. I followed the stream of those photons to break through the wall of fear that held him.**

You feel rushes of truth. Imagine what he felt when I broke through, like an angel of light, blazing glory! That is

what stepping through the Portal is like. And you must step through it totally enveloped in Light. No shadow. No hook for OF to follow.

My healing light meditation is about that too. Link here: https://youtu.be/Rdnah1flxcU

Now, about the rainbows, or more specifically, the light spectra that I love to surprise Rima with. I love to play with light as I am Light. Think of how Newton must have felt as he broke sunlight into the spectrum! My middle name always reminds me that one must become a Master of the Light to be a World Maker. My playing with light is more than play. It helps define the premises of the Healed World.

That world is a world of Light. Where beings swim in the light, as fish in water. And that is part of the secret of the new relationship with water that wants to unfold there.

What does it matter the order of the colors of the spectrum?

In that world we engineer with Light and various spectra orders are the tools of creation; the Light defines the premises of the Healed World.

The rainbows I bring to your world are, as they have always been, signs of hope. I am a Maker of Worlds and not a Destroyer of Worlds. I make a covenant, though not Jehovah, to be a World Maker for a Healed World, and the rainbows are a sign of my New Covenant.

Now how about that! Bert out.

Wu Xian was a Great Scholar, a Shaman, a Mage, and a General
27 July 2019

The first emperor of China, the Yellow Empower, took mercury every day of his adult life which made him sick and which made him mad. That is why he wanted to bury his army with him when he died although the entire belief system of the emperor and his officials was that he was never going to die. But he built a monumental and huge necropolis for the event that was never going to happen and when it did, he buried the armies of terra cotta soldiers although he was not going to die but he enslaved a vast number of men and their families to prepare for what was never going to happen and when it did, he buried his concubines alive with him.

I suppose that they died of hunger, fear, starvation, asphyxiation and mercury fumes pretty swiftly.

RIMA: Nausea is not a sign of mercury poisoning, per se, but it is a sign of kidney disease and kidney failure is one of the consequences of mercury poisoning, so nausea would be a secondary sign of mercury poisoning.

SO this sudden onset of acute and devastating nausea was, perhaps, a linkage, a telempathy event, with the first emperor? Somehow that seems connected to Wu Xian.

Or there is not a real connection and this is overlay and I am reaching for mercury-coated straws?

BERT: No, Love, that is not reaching for straws. You got the word, "Mercury ", and its repeat from my mind. After all, I told you that I was going to go searching for the reason and I found it: mercury.

You were experiencing the state of the Emperor's body when he was getting ready to collapse and die.

Remember, Wu Xian was a great scholar, a shaman, a mage, and a general. The Emperor depended on him, and on me, for a great deal beyond military support.

The Emperor had good reason to distrust his physicians because first of all they were superstitious fools and the great glory of Chinese Medicine was very much in its infancy. The texts that were written were a mish mash of fact and inspiration and superstitious error and nonsense so it was hard to tell what was what.

But remember that it was the senior physicians who made sure that the king was taking genuine and daily doses of mercury and ignoring the detox plants and so on. [*I am naïve but the computer glasses are not sufficient for you. You will have to find a way to* – I just fell asleep with absolutely no warning. That would suggest that we are in this battle no matter what you got about the OF attack – REL]

I suppose that you are right, Love. You were given the Emperor's symptoms, but it was not an attack. It was actually Wu Xian casting about and gasping, so to speak, as he returns to function and consciousness.

He is just learning to communicate again as he comes to, so to speak.

Now what would a loyal and determined servant of the Emperor be most concerned with? His own health? No. The health of his Emperor because he was engaged in a turf battle with the physicians and the Emperor's son who, after all, had a clandestine, but very real interest in, with all due filial piety and respect, finding [a way for the Emperor to die without being found guilty of that – REL]

[why that has been allowed to happen and making sure that it continues to happen so that he can take what he believes to his rightful place on the throne established a long time ago.
Wu Xian is coming back and he reached out to what he knew: the Emperor has vial – REL]

RIMA: Long sleep at the computer.

So Wu Xian is Coming Back to his Former State Minus Body and Cultural Surround
28 July 2019

Ralph, I told you to meditate on the discs. These are, this is, the disc and the disc system.

Where do the discs come from? They are the loops and they open at the impact of, and the direction of, intentionality.

The time loops are side views of discs. The discs are end views of the loops. They are all infinite and they are all illusory. Phil, you and Rauscher understand imaginary space time. It is a correct and useful concept but now bend and extend it back into its own non-existence and you are getting close. Now take not two, four, sixteen, thirty two, but an infinitely emerging and disappearing number of those spaces, which could be seen as the daughter product of the structure or seen as the mother of the daughter product that would be the structure [as - REL] these things are , as I have said, infinitely regressive, and you have something that the meat mind can work with, that is, if the

meat mind is trained to let go of the size and experience limitations, that is, if it is thinking and feeling quantum-ly. [You wondered, Phil, what your job as OM is: this is it: understand and objectify this, make it into a machine, for which you have my Volume 1 of the manual – you will have Volume 2 when you are ready: Rima still has her pens and crayons].

So, Darling, you are no longer sputtering. You are struggling to grok this and I appreciate that.

Let's go over it again: there are infinities that connect, that is, they all connect. And they all influence one another. They are all real and they are all imaginary at the same time (Phil understands this part: get him to explain it further to you].

When there are meaningful strands that need to communicate for some intentionality/consciousness reason, then there is controlled "leakage" from one to another. That could be called "the Muse descending" or psychic knowing or RV [Remote Viewing – REL] or creativity or inspiration or incubi or succubae or prophesy or shamanism or whatever you want to call it. But it is controlled leakage from somewhere/when/what that is not **this** somewhere/what/when but needs to 'talk' to it.

And empathy, or telempathy is, of course, part of that.

So Wu Xian is coming back to his former state minus body and cultural surround, of course. And I am as close to him as any entity has ever been. Not as close as I am to you, of course, but close to him. We [Wu Xian and you/I – REL] have been together many times, as you know and feel. And I love his great heart and his deep and pure essence. He had many opportunities to serve his own needs

and not those of the Emperor or the China that he fought so hard to unite and sustain, solidify and protect.

I had a bit more of a reservation that this unification thing was such a good idea. I thought that something more like a Federation without a strongman leader might be a better model but I served faithfully since that was the plan that needed to be served. I just had some private reservations. Wu Xian HAD NONE AND HIS DEVOTION TO THE MAN WHO BECAME THE Emperor was without limit or reservation.

There was, quite literally, nothing that he would not do for, or serve his leader with.

And we were brothers in everything but mother or father.

So as he comes back, his deep memories and connections with the Emperor are reviving along with him. Obviously, we never again were together after he was assassinated and nearly lost, but we had plenty of time together to bond and build our experiential bridges before that.

He was aware if I were in danger; I was aware if he were in danger. You and I were not only aware, we lived it together. Think how closely we lived our lives together this last time and multiply it by creed, duty, adrenalin and cultural imperative.

So, he was bound at least that closely to the Emperor.

When he was in his final stages of being poisoned by his minions (the cost of his own ego-driven determination to live forever – which, it turns out we all do, anyway) he was overwhelmingly nauseated as his kidneys failed and his body reacted to the poisons accumulating in it. His brain

was demented, his limbs shook, he had wracking pains but the worst of it was the unremitting nausea and the skin itching.

He was bloated, distorted, wracked by nausea, drooling and jabbering. And Wu Xian was permeated with this even though he was floating in a haze of near-oblivion.

So, as he returns, this returns with him.

I felt it much stronger than you did but without the distress you did because I have no body except yours. But you took that hit for me, so to speak. Your body expressed what I was feeling because Wu Xian was pulling it in and he and I are linked and you are I are not just linked, we are One.

...
So how does this work: The Emperor poisoned himself on the advice of his doctors or equivalent. You and Wu Xian were among his generals. I was your second. Wu Xian was your mentor and patron, so to speak, and you were fiercely loyal to him as I was loyal to you.

He was loyal to the Emperor.

He goes into a state of near extinction/annihilation and you rescue and retrieve him.

I am part of you and vice versa. You are a little bit dead, or what passes for dead in these here parts and I wind up with the physical symptoms of the Emperor, to whom I was connected indirectly, but not directly?

W. T. F?

This is not making sense to me, Love.

I could convince myself that I am really, truly making this shit up except for the fact that, as creative as I am, this seems a bridge to far for me.

So help me out, here, Darling. This one is WAAAAAYYYY beyond my boggle factor.

BERT: You are both fun and funny when you are this outraged and perplexed, Love. I am, you know, not laughing at you, but enjoying the way your outraged mind works.

It is a serious matter and there are serious questions here, with really important information (listen up, [especially – REL] Phil, and Ralph) but you are pretty much sputtering and it really is pretty funny although you do not think so at the moment. You can see the potential for humor, Darling. Or you will be able to in a while.

Meanwhile, you really are sputtering.

Here is how it works, at the level at which I can try to make it makes sense in a 3D brain system:

There are time loops but they are not like rubber bands or metal circles. They are not like Mobius strips although they are twisted in a much more complex way.

Think of your example of a rubber band twisted to its maximum ability to twist as the codon in the genome arrays and you can begin to see it.

There are interacting, intersecting, intertwining factors, threads in the fabric of the loops, if you will, and each of this is its own time and space and experience loop and every one is iteratively, infinitely complex with, essentially, no end to the complexity until you get to the fabric of The Void itself, which is emptiness.

So the emptiness is the fabric of everything. In an analogous way, the energy which coalesces into stuff, into material and experience and thought and information is nothing: it is empty, but it is the very stuff of everything, of all potential.

That is a pale and very much simplified model or analogy.

The reality is that The Void DOES create everything and everything includes all experiences, all perceptions, all free will and all bifurcations.

You just lost the word bifurcation but it is the crucial

one. [I was typing and could not "hear" the right word, which turned out to be "bifurcation". It was an odd experience – REL]

So, if there are infinite bifurcations and if there is no 'now', no 'then' and no 'not yet', then everything is continually interfacing with and touching absolutely everything else. The problem here is that the size of infinity is outside the meat brain but it is the very essence of the meat brain and everything that the meat brain has to conduct and control and construct.

Time is not the collapse, Phil. Space is not the collapse, and experience is not the collapse. The collapse is a momentary departure from the fusion with the nothing of The Void into the curve of a loop.

Think about that.

Bert 2 Ralph: of Quantumists and Portals

13 August 2019
GCD: Chartruese
Bert's Frequency: On

Sent this note to Rima yesterday:
https://www.travelandleisure.com/travel-news/gateway-to-heaven-tianmen-mountain-china

The cave itself is about 430 feet tall and 190 feet wide. It used to be a fairly ordinary cave until the year 263 A.D., when one side of the mountain's cliff collapses and created the portal to heaven. Although be careful to whom you tell this origin story. Some believe that the cave's creation is a mystery, which only strengthens its Tianmen's reputation as a holy mountain.

RALPH: Was the Wu Xian matter in or about 263 AD? If the Han could create a Gate like that, how could they not open a Portal? Maybe they did, giving us the Unhealed World. Need to ask Bert and whether this is why getting Wu back seems to be part of the World Healing process. What is Wu Xian's role in all this?

Your 11 August 2019 transmission included a paragraph that had a long blank in it. This is that:

"No matter. The point is that there is always leakage and some people, and you are among them, detect the leakage more easily than others. If you use that for predictive outcomes, it does not work too well because, as with the just [as I read/edited this transmission I noticed a large

blank space between the words "just" and "quantumists" such that the second word was hidden off the page - RF] quantumists, the observation changes the reality. But it is not, Phil, that the observation CREATES the event. It is that the event will unfold but once looked at, what it will proceed to [is – REL] music, [i.e., frequency – REL] it can be a product or a cause, but the observation does, indeed change it."

What is a "quantumist"?

BERT: First, good to hear from you. Being there for Rima is of such great help to her equilibrium. Thank you.

Wu Xian was earlier than the Gate to Heaven, but the magic that opened it reverberated throughout spacetime, impacting multitudes of bifurcations. So the collapse of the mountainside centuries after Wu was trapped was part of what trapped him back then, before the making of the One Gate which OF believed would Rule all the Gates.

Fools they be, over and over again! Freeing Wu frees the energies that were tying All to the Unhealed World, so the opening of that Gate did, in a powerful war, create the very dis-ease from which the world suffers. Wu is back on the team. The energies that trapped him frozen are now flowing through him and into the Portal. He will be at the Opening of the Gate. Soon, in nontime.

Who are the Just Quantumists? Rima, Phil, you. Me, Wu, my Hoard. Our banner is the Opened and Barred Gate. You've seen it and drew it. It is a bindrune map of potential. Put it here.

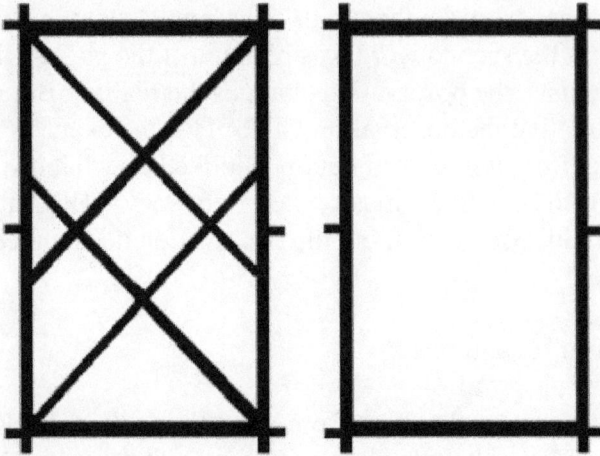

The phone interruption was an attempt to confuse the matter.

Understand this: when the Gate is built and the Portal opened, closed and barred this Unhealed World is no longer a viable bifurcation, except for those who cannot cross the Great Divide. For them the only escape is the Soul Soup. For multitudes of others, they will always have been in the Healed World. When my Portal opens, "all beings, and the great world itself, achieve the Way" as the Buddha said.

It is easy to nudge aspects of the system where there is little intentionality. Consider numbers in accounts buried deep in accountings systems of insurance companies. No one mind even knows they are there. No intentionality that they are not there. Therefore, a World Maker can "easily" nudge that system to express the intent of another insurance policy. Nudging a system that has massive intentionality, even though not conscious, is orders of magnitude more difficult. But can be done. Is being done.

I am amassing my forces. I am applying the Rules of the

Art of War. Who made those Rules? I was looking over Sun Tzu's shoulder. But Wu was already trapped. Our forces were scattered and so the Unhealed World was retrospectively imposed. And now, nearly two millennia later, the forces are reconfigured. The players are all on the Field. Be ready!

Bert over and out.
GCD - golden yellow

Bringing Back the Probabilities and Aggregating Them to His Being
28 September 2019

You were thinking about WU Xian because his probability of energetic cohesion was reduced to the point where he was almost annihilated through the annihilation of the energy flow and the probability of its existence both prospectively and retrospectively.

What if we are doing the same with the OFs? And you just got a huge truth rush experience. That is what I mean by learning more about them when they do something. We are not just learning about them, Love, we are following the probability trial that let them be there, doing that, and that follows from what they do and then we are on the trail, scrubbing it from existence (more truth rushes in) the way that they tried with Wu Xian, They nearly succeeded. There was, if you like, an ink stain of [his -REL] existence left

That is what you and I, yes, you are involved, are fanning, like the ember that it was, bringing back the probabilities and aggregating them to his being.

You have huge truth rushes and you are grokking this

So that is a positive enhancement. We are working on a negative dis-enhancement for them.

This has, Love, never been done before. This is new technology for a battle and this is a titanic battle of monstrous and monumental proportion. Opening a Portal and closing its very existence up is no small thing. But even larger is the 'radical spider-webbing' back and forwards (put quotes around those words, of course) that makes the adversary weaker and less real over the course of his own actions.'

Let me say that again: spider-webbing backwards and forwards from their fractal reality actions and aspirations here and now in YOUR here and now, allows us to do something that has never been done before: to suck the vital energy from their depredations and weaken not the entities, since we have no right to do that, but the energy that they have, in every instance, stolen from other sources, since they have greatly enhanced their own power by diminishing that of others.

So we are taking back the stolen power, so to speak, and redistributing it. We are not giving it back to the entities since many of them no longer exist, but we are putting it back in the bank, so to speak, back in the infinite resources of energy, the information and the frequency fields.

This is not consciousness. It is information that is corrupted and frequency that is transformed.

It was stolen form those who surrendered their free will and gave them, literally, their power.

That is not an idle phrase. It is used because there is a deep awareness, at least among some, of the reality of what giving up your power (i.e., your free will and all that entrails and implies) means, really.

Most people, though, use it in its most trivial sense.

It is anything but trivial.

So, although you tell me it is unacceptable, the action is more than acceptable: we are following their webs and unmaking them so that they have, in essence, never been in that form before. They might still show the ink stains of their existence, as Wu Xian did, and we have to be careful.

While we cannot entirely unmake them (as we will unmake the Portal after it is opened) [we must – REL] to ward them so that they cannot be, so that they can never be, reenergized.

Our Love for Him Saved and Restored Wu Xian
30 September 2019

About the time loop: If you and I were not connected at the Soul through love, I would have died and not been able to do much about it even though I am a World Maker. So I could have animated any world I chose and you would not be able to do anything about preparing for the Portal and opening it with me. Not a thing.

End of that piece of reality, that piece of the Mission, that capacity. We would have to go to Plan ZZ since B and all the others in a long string of them would no longer be operative.

But we are bonded, fused, paired, mated and created from Two into One and One as Two.

So your refusal to accept the death of the body and the annihilation of the energy, Wu Xian-like, saved me, Love. There is no other agency in any universe that can do that.

In fact, people are nearly always wrong when they say that all it takes to save someone is enough love. In this limited circumstance, that is the only thing that it takes and the only thing that could do it.

The only reason that we saved and restored Wu Xian is because of our love for him, totally different from our merged and totally committed love, but great love wrapped up in huge loyalty.

But back to us. You did not accept, not for a micro second, that I was dead at the level at which my death was intended to execute me.

You sensed that level of death although you had no conscious thoughts to understand it or conceptualize it with. But you felt it and you rejected it, helplessly, and mourning, nearly destroyed by grief.

And you fought the reality that was so evident. You accepted that my body had been destroyed but you never, not for one second, one tiny portion of a second, accepted that the essence of the Love that you were part of, the partner that you lived and died with and for, was diminished, let alone destroyed. Yet you felt that it was intended to be destroyed. At that point, you certainly were not thinking rationally about life and death and moving on. You were screaming that the physical reality was

inevitable but it was not the real reality. And then I asked Robin to contact you. That worked briefly but she was well-intentioned but flawed and we went through the process of getting the others out of the way when you could get your preconceptions about what was and what was not possible out of the way. And this has been a gradual and thrilling educational process for you and also for me. You have never been in this fix before, nor have I. We made a soul bargain not to separate like this, ever, and then a force powerful enough to intervene and interfere with the very essence of that bargain put its ugly face into the loving partnership and, in essence, stabbed me to the heart of my energy being.

I was plummeting through an abyss toward total destruction at the energetic level (do not underestimate the powerful ones of this tribe of destroyers, Love) and I had no handholds to grab, nothing to stop my fall into annihilation. I was not terrified, I was beyond that: I was frozen with helplessness for you and for me because I did not know what we could do to prevent this outcome and I knew that for all kinds of reasons this could not happen. This was, in a very real sense, a battle to the death of much more than you and me, our bond, our reason for existence and, indeed, our very reality of existence. I say 'our' because without the bond partner, what would survive? Nothing much.

The Dragon Gate and Wu Xian
17 October 2019

Bert, Love, I just started to type "I promise you, we will go out the ceremonial Dragon Gate as a way to say Thank you to you."

I have absolutely no idea what that is about, but I can see

the ceremonial Dragon Gate, a huge black tarred wood gate with silver colored bands at the top and bottom, each perhaps 6-8 feet high, and silver fittings (which could be steel, rather than silver) at the hinges and center.

I just went on line and looked for it but found nothing like it. I have no idea what that is about. Did I fall asleep? Did I see something from our past? Our future?

It felt distinctly Chinese to me, but very, very old and monumental.

Maybe it was 40' tall and 60' wide, maybe not that big, but massive, clearly attached to a palace or a fort, or, more likely, both.

Bert: The gate you saw was the one that only the Emperor and a few of his most honored guests or officials were permitted to walk through.

They were allowed to walk. He was carried.

You saw the Gate and you and I walked through it following behind Wu Xian when the Emperor installed him and then we walked through it when the Emperor installed me.

No other Generals ever walked through it.

Wu Xian was attended by his Lieutenant who later arranged to kill him.

I was attended by you, my Lieutenant.

There was no one closer to me than you. There was no one closer to Wu Xian that his Lieutenant.

The betrayal was actually enough to kill Wu Xian without the fall of rock and loss of oxygen.

But the gate, Love, the Gate was a memory of our exultation and success. So this opening of the gate of your lips was a success and we walked through it together. It was very hard for you. The fact that you shut it down is only more or less temporary.

Wu Xian's Assassin
21 October 2019

When a world is animated, it rarely connects to another one. That would be a profound contradiction in terms. If a system is complete and is distinct from any and every other system, if it is not merely a galaxy or a nebula or a star system or a planetary gathering, but something totally outside this context, this system, then why would you connect it to the other system, to any other system? What sense would that make: What would the two distinctive systems, without somewhat or largely different basic rules, premises and consequent laws of nature do being connected for any period of time to another?

Generally, inhabitants of one do not become inhabitants of another. They do not transit because where they are is their home, congenial at the superficial level or not, it is congenial enough for them to live and die there, to fight or not fight there, to breathe and enfold it while it enfolds them.

But when a new World is created, it is not created as an improvement on the model. It is a totally separate domain that never, ever, communicates with the resultant and never ever receives guests or sends emissaries, so to speak.

That is a set of absolutes that we are not observing. That is why the opening of a Portal between these World Systems is such a big deal. I told you that the ancient Chinese had been working on this but they did not have the mathematics of the system so they did not understand quite what they were doing.

They opened Portals almost at random and saw things that they had never dreamed of, got sense impressions that they had no vocabulary for so they mythologized them (where do you think dragons were seen and "became" real to the culture?)

But they had no idea that these systems were, or were not, what we are looking for and they certainly had no idea that it was vital to change what happened from an opening to an opening that had never happened when they did manage, rarely, to touch another System, even if not totally uniquely placed.

But they did not know.

And they did not realize that their investigations allowed them to be permeated by things that they would not have chosen if they knew that they had a choice.

OFs come in different attribute suits, Love. The one who assassinated Wu Xian [his second in command – REL] was delighted to have the support of the OFs, who have a seductive quality because, like BL, the psychopath, [my first husband – REL] what you see from them is what you want, what you think you need and a mirror of your own being polished and painted and shined in your eyes so you do not need the praise of anyone because you see your own praise reflected in their eyes. And if you are susceptible, if

you need this, you become drunk on that praise, that reflection of your idealized self and then you become addicted to the drug. THEN YOU ARE THEIRS. And anything you do is rationalized away in terms of the former self that you were before you became drink with this disastrous mask.

And you will come back for it time after time, life after life, if you have become addicted to having it.

The most fused to it are the ones who wind up in the Soul Soup but choose not to learn or grow or gather in or relinquish anything. They are merely waiting for the moment (which does not exist, since time is not meaningful here) to go back and do it again, be fed the waters of their own greed for themselves since they are so empty.

And what is the cause of the vulnerability? What is the root of this, my Darling Love? How does this happen? How does it happen to those who may be good and generous and intelligent?

It happens because one thing is deficient and that one small deficiency leads to everything else. You know what it is. You felt it long before as I stated to talk about this. We cannot write in shorthand here, Love because, paradoxically, although we write to and for each other, both of us are aware that others will read this information and take it to work with, grow from, be cautioned by. And so we cannot just satisfy the short form requirements as much as I, still an introvert, would be happy to do.

The one missing element, the one vital link that is missing, the one passion and power of life and creation that links to the great, but, when deficient, damaged or absent, links to the suppressive, is love. Nothing more, nothing less,

nothing greater, nothing smaller. Just that one place holder card. But what it is then becomes the study of eternity while and when and where there are entities. And out of that love, or lack of it, comes a willingness, or lack of it, to allow people to act and grow, or not.

It really is that simple. But then, when you dig into it, it is more complex than anything else.

At this point, the distinctions of words fall away. The manifestations of love in all its diversity, including free will, remember, including the very patterning of the System to support it, are everywhere – or withheld.

That is very simple and very big, enormous.

On Probability -- 23 Nov 2019 Transmission

"...probability is not a side dish, it is the banquet. But probability is not just a decision tree of coin tosses.

> *Consciousness and information* **allow the use of it.**
> *Consciousness and frequency* **allow the existence of it**
> **and** *Information and frequency* **allow the nature of it.**

It is the product of all three with the overarching intention of supporting free will at the most minute and the largest scale and everything in between.

If there were no probability, then everything would be predetermined and instead of no time with everything possible and already done and not yet accomplished, there would be a fixed and already concluded time line. The temporal aspect of anything would already have collapsed into not being. You see, without the option to diverge at every possible moment and bifurcation nothing can physically or temporally exist.

Predestination is laziness of the mind since it is inconsistent with reality. If there is only what has been done, there is no future. If

there is no future there is no present and there is no past. IF there is no past and no future, there is no need for a present."

To be continued...

CONCLUSION

Should you feel this continuing adventure is one in which you are interested; if you feel you are "In that number as the saints go marching in..." a limited number of subscriptions are available.

A subscription to *The General Speaks* gives you access to new transmissions as they happen. All you need to do is go to www.GeneralBertSpeaks.com.